Tightrope Tango

Blessings on Your
Big Life!

Ray Watson

Tightrope Tango

Unleashing the Power of Balance Between Work and Life

Ray Waters

PRESCIENT BOOKS

Tightrope Tango

Unleashing the Power of Balance Between Life and Work

Second Edition

Library of Congress Control Number
2013939896

ISBN
978-0-9893553-1-5

First Printing 2013

To my best friend and wife Jane – getting to tango
with you has been the great joy of my life.
Your genuine goodness, quiet strength and infectious smile
bless me more than you could ever know.
I am honored to get to walk this road
with you by my side.

Table of Contents

Foreword
General Philip M. Breedlove, USAF

Tightrope Tango is a must read for people on the go who are interested in finding ways to live a healthier and more productive life. Whether you are a C-suite leader, midlevel manager or launching a new career, *Tightrope Tango* can reinforce old, or build new techniques and habits to help immunize you from the pressures of daily life. As Ray points out, it is really about knowing what your "big rocks" are and finding ways to keep them all in balance.

Considering the demands we all face, taking time to reflect and truly understand what is important is a monumental first step. Ray make clever use of storytelling to guide you through the lives of characters Clayton and Darlene, a husband and wife who have lost sight of priorities and don't realize they are close to the edge.

While entertaining and easy to read, the authors challenge readers with exercises to illicit deeper thought and reflection. *Tightrope Tango* is a brilliant self-help tool that addresses comprehensive fitness and provides insightful and useful suggestions that can help you realize the "power of balance."

Acknowledgements

We would like to thank the following people
who have made this project possible.

Rick Griffin – Your enthusiasm for the project and advice
shared during the first draft was greatly appreciated.

Stephanie Chan – Your wise assistance in shaping
the analytical component of *Tightrope Tango*
made this a much stronger book.

Bill Hybels, Pastor, Willowcreek Community Church –
Your talk given at the Global Leadership Summit became the
inspiration for our chapter on emotional health and well-
being. Our Reverend Shadinger is based on the lessons you
taught that day. Thank you for the great contribution you are
making to leaders around the world.

Kaitlyn Tabares – Your impeccable proofreading, good
eyes and insightful suggestions were appreciated and made
concluding this project relatively painless.

The congregations of The Village –
So many of you are already modeling the principles
found in this book. Watching you live healthy balanced
lives inspires us daily.

Ray

Introduction

Tightrope Tango is many things: a culmination of over 60 years working with the community, the result of extensive experience speaking with people from all walks of life, and a simple story with the aim of inspiring practical change. Above all, *Tightrope Tango* is a collection of principles that can be utilized in both the workplace and at home.

Think of these principles as an overhaul of the workflow efficiency of your life – once applied, they will make it possible for you to restore the delicate balance between the things you want and the things you need.

The main thrust of this book is to help you ascertain inefficiencies and target them with easy-to-use solutions and exercises. Knowing is half the battle, and once you target the parts of your daily habits that are holding you back, you'll be able to work toward changing them for the better.

Who should read *Tightrope Tango*?

Balance is important, whether you are a boardroom executive who just can't seem to find time for the family or you are a newbie associate who is struggling to get into the swing of things. Tightrope Tango seeks to provide a framework for self-analysis for professionals at all levels.

How can *Tightrope Tango* help my career?

It is true that *Tightrope Tango* offers many solutions for analyzing your personal life. How then, you may ask, can these solutions also apply to the workplace?

The answer is simple and can be discovered in the following pages. The crux of the matter is without balance at home and at your job, life can become quite overwhelming. Personal problems invariably leak into the workplace. The stress of maintaining and advancing a career puts a strain on the home life, which in turn affects your work, which then affects your home life, and so on and so forth. It is a vicious cycle that this book seeks to help you end.

On top of helping you find a happy balance between work and home, *Tightrope Tango* also helps you develop a different perspective and presents solutions aimed toward managing personnel more effectively. Healthy well balanced employees are much more productive employees.

These analytical tools are powerful no matter what field you are in – marketing, law, business, or otherwise. You will learn how to communicate effectively and confidently, and you will learn how to organize and manage what is essentially the "workflow" of your life.

How to use *Tightrope Tango*

The principles in *Tightrope Tango* are best used in conjunction with one another. It is recommended that you read through the entire book and revisit exercises that are particularly useful for you. Each exercise is designed to be adaptable to your needs, featuring open-ended questions and encouraging self-analysis rather than one-size-fits-all solutions. Once you finish the entire course of exercises in *Tightrope Tango*, you will have developed keen problem-solving skills that are applicable in all areas of your life.

Why is *Tightrope Tango* written as a story?

Just as most textbooks and technical manuals may offer examples and hypothetical situations, so does *Tightrope Tango* utilize this technique to demonstrate the principles of leading a balanced life. Though the characters in the story may not have a direct parallel to the people you know, there are several reasons for framing the exercises in such a manner:

- A mnemonic device. By structuring it as a story, the principles will be easier to remember.

- Principles in action. Simply brainstorming solutions for the issues in your own life does not paint a complete picture. In *Tightrope Tango*, you will see how universal principles can be applied to your own situation.

- A holistic view. The principles of *Tightrope Tango*, while adaptable to your personal needs, are best used together to form the foundation of new habits. The story clearly demonstrates how changes can be effected to benefit all areas of your life.

As you are taking the journey with our heroes Clayton and Darlene, exercises and suggested solutions will follow every section of the story. You will learn how to target problem areas in your life and re-evaluate your priorities.

Tightrope Tango is the first book in a series that focuses on powerful self-analysis tools for the work and home.

The Balancing Act

"I don't have any more time, Darlene!" Clayton said.

Darlene looked exasperated. "It just doesn't make sense. Why can't you go to Eddie's game tomorrow? You're his father, and he notices when you are not there."

"If I don't have evening appointments, I can't sell," Clayton explained to his wife. "If I don't sell, there won't be a promotion – ever. If my income doesn't go up, who's going to pay for your pretty car, your jewelry, your antiques, your spa treatments and all the other expensive crap you like to buy?"

"That's not fair!" Darlene declared. "You know that the only reason I buy any of those things is because I want our family to have the very best."

"Sure," Clayton said sarcastically. "You're bankrupting us. When we finally crash, I just hope you don't mind raising Eddie in a rundown doublewide."

Clayton knew how to end an argument with his wife. He watched as she blinked away a tear. He realized the cruel reference to her childhood home was tacky and way over the line, but there was no time for apologies now.

She shook her head in disgust and walked back into the bathroom to continue getting ready for work. He quickly gathered his paperwork and laptop off the kitchen table, got into his car and headed for the office.

My life really sucks, Clayton thought as he lit a cigarette – one of many he would smoke this day. *Why am I even married? Living with that woman is way more stressful than it is supposed to be. How'd we get ourselves into such a mess?*

Clayton James' life had started like a fairy tale. He had grown up with a natural ability to throw a baseball. It had earned him a great amount of attention in high school and then a full ride to Gardner Webb University in North Carolina. After college, Clayton played two more years of ball with the Kane County Cougars, a Low A minor league team in Geneva, Illinois.

Life seemed very manageable for the affable young man. There had been talk that Clayton would pitch in the big leagues and he probably would have had he not heard the *big pop*. While pitching on a breezy summer day in Clayton's second year at Geneva, he heard a sound like a gunshot go off inside his shoulder and realized he had thrown his last professional pitch. In an instant, Clayton understood his baseball dream was over. A pitcher doesn't come back from a torn labrum.

Always an optimist, when his baseball life ended, Clayton threw himself into finding a suitable career. After surveying his options, he secured an upwardly mobile job in the investment industry and began dating a beautiful young woman named Darlene.

Darlene Card, petite with dark brown hair, had grown up 100 miles from Chicago. A former high school cheerleader, she had earned her degree in speech therapy from Roosevelt University. After graduation, she landed a very exciting and challenging job at Children's Memorial Hospital in Chicago.

It was the fairy tale again. Handsome man marries a beautiful woman and begins living the American dream. Two years after their marriage, their son, Charles Edward James, was born. Clayton, Darlene, and Eddie looked like the perfect American family.

Lately, it seemed like their world was unraveling all around them.

A near collision on the Kennedy Expressway caused Clayton to hit his brakes quickly, startling him back to the present.

As traffic began to flow again, Clayton wondered, *Where did it all go so wrong?* Clayton and Darlene loved each other very much but the stress of their jobs and raising an eight year old son had become way more difficult than they had imagined. Clayton looked at many of his peers and superiors at his company and they all seemed to handle their lives so much better than he did. He never had enough time to do the things he needed to do. That, along with Darlene's spending habits, had nearly put him over the edge.

When was the last time we really had fun together? Clayton was blank on that one. *Little wonder the doctor is concerned about my blood pressure. Oh well, maybe I should play the lottery. I've got to have some relief.*

Analysis

"It's incredibly easy to get caught up in an activity trap, in the busyness of life, to work harder and harder at climbing the ladder of success only to discover it's leaning against the wrong wall. It is possible to be busy-very busy — without being very effective."
STEPHEN COVEY

Keep in mind that Clayton and Darlene are only an example of the struggles you may deal with in your own life. Perhaps in your situation, both you and your spouse are heavy spenders – whether it's on the latest technological gadget or eating out at restaurants. Or perhaps spending isn't your problem at all; maybe you are struggling with a time deficit and you can never catch your breath. Or perhaps you just moved to a new city and are having trouble finding opportunities to develop a social circle. The list goes on.

More importantly, our example illustrates how easy it is to get stuck in a rut. One thing leads to another, and before you know it, the same things are causing trouble day in and day out. Our goal in this part of the analysis is to make sure the cracks in the sidewalk don't become enormous potholes, so to speak.

Can you think of things that you are unhappy with in your personal life?

Problems to solve	Solutions
ex. constant clutter in apartment	

TIGHTROPE TANGO

The first step, as in any analysis, is to determine what the issues are. Just as you may begin a project by listing goals and obstacles, so you should approach your personal life. In later sections, we will discuss how to discover the root causes and also how to create lasting strategies to effect permanent change.

The Invitation

Clayton was still thinking about his earlier conversation with Darlene as he pulled his black Lexus sedan into the parking lot of F.C. MAPLES.

F.C. MAPLES, a financial investment firm where Clayton had worked for the last eight years, was named for Fred Charles Maples, an octogenarian billionaire who founded the company 46 years ago. Maples was a living legend in Chicago.

Maples had an unusual story. He had not been groomed from childhood for his success. He had grown up in a very poor family with no plans of going to college or of pursuing a career in business. However, everything changed for Maples when he was 20 years old.

Through a strange twist of events, Maples had decided after an especially inspiring church meeting to try college. Having never been a very good student, after just one semester, Maples and the university both determined he did not have the skills necessary to continue. However, one college administrator saw something very special in the young man and encouraged him to not give up but to pursue his dreams, whatever they might be. Maples listened to the administrator and took his second chance at education and never looked back, graduating at the top of his class.

Now eighty-two years old, Fred C., as he was affectionately called, still spent two or three days a week in his 54th floor office at the corner of Michigan and Vine.

Maples was known throughout the country as one of the most productive business success stories in American history. He had been a great insurance agent and investment broker in his early years and then became a successful CEO without ever losing his smile and his reputation for having a good heart.

Fred C. led his company with a loving but firm hand. His company's interviewing procedures were grueling, but they had produced a firm of very successful overachievers who possessed many of the values Maples held dear.

Maples was a rare CEO who really cared about the total health and well-being of all the people who worked for him. Because he was innovative in his interaction with employees, his company was voted one of the top 10 companies to work for in the Chicago area.

As Clayton arrived at work, he walked into the office revealing little or none of the stress he had felt on his commute. He had a sanguine personality, and his natural optimism caused him to say to himself, *This just might be the day I figure out my life.*

Just before 9:00 AM, Sandy, Clayton's assistant for the last three years, stepped inside his office and reported, "Clayton, Mr. Maple's secretary just called and said he would like to meet with you and Darlene tonight at 7:00 PM for dinner at his house. She wants to know if that will be a problem."

"A problem? Absolutely not. Tell Mr. Maples we will be there." Clayton was stunned. *Why would Maples want Darlene and me to meet with him? It must be a promotion.* His mind was spinning fast as he called Darlene to discuss the evening and make plans for someone to watch Eddie.

"Hey, sweetheart," Clayton said, ignoring the harsh exit of just 90 minutes ago.

"Hi. How are you?" Darlene's voice was cool, but Clayton was not surprised.

"Honey, I'm sorry about this morning, but I have some good news now." Clayton was in his best sales mode.

"Great," Darlene replied. "I can't wait to hear what's going to come out of your mouth. You are always so encouraging to me."

"Stop being so sarcastic. This sounds huge. Mr. Maples wants to meet with you and me tonight at his house. Can you arrange for your mom to keep Eddie? I think it might be a big promotion."

Clayton felt the momentum possibly changing with Darlene and her hurt feelings.

"That's great honey," Darlene said, slightly more syrupy than Clayton thought was normal, "but I have a staff meeting tonight at the hospital."

"Skip it. Tell 'em you're sick."

"My job's important too, you know."

"Look, you don't just get invited to Fred C. Maples' house on a whim." Clayton said. "This is a big deal! If this is the promotion I think it is, you might even be able to quit your job all together."

"Great! Then I'd have time to spend even more money."

Darlene ended the call without saying goodbye.

Oh, well, Clayton thought. *She'll get over it.* The rest of the day sailed by quickly as Clayton thought about his meeting with Mr. Maples and the possible promotion that awaited him.

Analysis

"When the urgent crowds out the important, people urgently accomplish nothing of value."

- ORRIN WOODWARD

"Being overwhelmed is often as unproductive as doing nothing, and is far more unpleasant. Being selective and 'doing less' is the path of the productive. Focus on the important few and ignore the rest."

- TIMOTHY FERRISS

Now that you have a list of things you are unhappy about, think about who else is involved in these problems. Think about whether or not your problems affect other people, such as a partner, family member or co-worker.

One of the most powerful tools you can tap into is your support network, whether it's your co-workers or your family. You will discover how important it is to have people pulling for you to discover and become your best self.

For instance, take a relationship between a supervisor and a subordinate. Mutual trust and communication are necessary for such a working relationship to flourish.

In this section, Clayton and Darlene are still floundering due to unresolved issues. They aren't sitting down and working through their problems together. Instead of talking to each other, they are talking at each other. Instead of working together as a team, each person feels as though they are unappreciated and ignored.

Similar situations can arise in both personal and working relationships. One of the foundations of successful team-building is ensuring that everyone is on the same page. Answer the following questions and be honest with yourself.

1. Are you more of a talker or a listener?

   _____

2. Are there any people in your life with whom you have difficulty communicating?

   _____
   _____
   _____
   _____

3. What problems generally arise when you attempt to communicate?

   _____
   _____
   _____
   _____

4. What are steps you can take to increase the effectiveness of your communication?

   _____
   _____
   _____
   _____

5. Is there anyone in your life with whom you wish you were closer?

_____

_____

_____

_____

6. How can you improve your relationship with these people?

_____

_____

_____

_____

The Challenge

As they pulled into the Maples' driveway, Clayton put out his cigarette and squeezed Darlene's hand for good luck.

"I don't like lying to my boss, you know?" Darlene said.

"I promise you our life will be better after tonight," Clayton said. He felt good about his prospects. He had no idea how right he was going to be.

Clayton and Darlene had been to Maples' house on two other occasions, but neither visit was very personal. A couple of years ago, all the employees with young children had come to the estate for a big Easter egg hunt, and last year, Clayton's work group had stopped by to look at Christmas decorations and enjoy some eggnog and holiday music. Tonight was going to be way different from anything Clayton and Darlene expected.

At 6:57 PM, Clayton rang the bell at Mr. Maples' palatial home. They were greeted by Toni, the Maples' longtime cook and housekeeper, who took Clayton and Darlene's jackets and led them into a magnificent sitting room. The room had two focal points. At one end was an impressive, stacked fieldstone fireplace which supported three massive mahogany beams that traversed the length of the room. The structure was masculine and inspiring. At first glance, it was easy to see this house was extraordinary.

On the opposite end of the room was an aquarium that served as a dividing wall between the sitting room and Maples' study. It held fish that looked more beautiful than anything Clayton and Darlene had ever seen. The layout of the tank, the clear water, and the schools of exotic fish created a tranquil, yet deeply moving sight.

Darlene noticed that Clayton was mesmerized by a purple octopus that seemed to effortlessly navigate a maze of live coral at one end of the aquarium.

"Cool, huh?" she asked.

"You think our lives would be easier if we had eight arms and legs?" Clayton said.

"Together, we already do," she replied.

"Yeah, I guess so. If only we could get them in sync like that octopus..."

At precisely 7:00 PM, in walked Fred C. Maples. He greeted the young couple warmly and thanked them for coming on such short notice.

In a moment, his wife entered the room and Maples' countenance lit up as if he were seeing her for the very first time. Fred C. always called her True Love. This is how friends and family and people from work addressed her. Her birth name was Elizabeth, but she hadn't heard that name in 60 years. She was Fred C.'s true love, and the name fit. True Love was a small woman with beautiful white hair. Nearly 80, she was striking. The feature everyone talked about long after leaving her presence was her radiant smile.

As Mr. and Mrs. Maples engaged the young couple in small talk, Clayton thought about his boss. The most magnetic man Clayton had ever met, Fred C. Maples was a strongly built man, even at his age. He had brilliant blue eyes that sparkled when he talked. Although he was worth several billion dollars, he never thought himself better than anyone. Clayton and Darlene both felt warm and at home in his presence.

　　　　　　　　　　　　　　TIGHTROPE TANGO

After a few moments of pleasantries, the Maples invited them into the small dining room to eat. They also had a larger dining room that could seat fifty guests. This smaller dining room was not as intimidating and made the evening feel even more comfortable.

Fred C. continued his small talk for a few moments as the soup was served and then changed the whole tone of the evening with a single question, "What do you two want out of this life?" It was a little abrupt but not rude. "I'm serious," the old man said. "What do you two want from this life?"

Clayton began, "I guess we want what everybody wants: a healthy family, a comfortable home, a secure job, and some good friends. That's about it."

The question had surprised Clayton, and he was not sure if he had answered very thoughtfully.

"What about you, Darlene?" the old man asked.

"I think about the same thing that Clayton said. I want to grow old and be happy about my life and what we achieved as a family," Darlene answered.

Maples nodded. "I see much potential in you, Clayton. You work hard, seem to love your brilliant and charming life partner, and you are mildly interested in sports, just like I am."

They all laughed. It was no secret that Maples loved sports. He almost bought the Cubs a few years earlier from the Tribune Company, but decided at the last moment that he would prefer to be Chicago's biggest fan rather than a sports franchise owner.

Maples was aware of Clayton's two-year minor league career before joining the company.

"The book on you as a player was you were tough and tenacious," Maples said. "Your commitment to make it to the top would have gotten you there had you not blown out your shoulder. That's why I knew you had potential to make it in the corporate world."

"Thank you, sir. That means a lot coming from you," Clayton replied.

Toni appeared with a pitcher of tea and refilled everyone's crystal glasses.

Maples took a sip of tea and then looked Clayton in the eyes.

"I'm getting to be an old man so let me cut straight to the chase. Clayton, I believe you might be heading towards a crash in business and in your family life."

Clayton felt as if he had just been politely kicked in the stomach.

"Excuse me, sir?" Clayton said, asking for a little more clarity.

"Clayton and Darlene, I hope you will listen to me. I believe you can accomplish any and everything you have ever hoped or dreamed. However, without balance in your life, you are heading for a serious train wreck."

Maples went on, passionate about what he was saying. "Thriving in the corporate world is similar to doing a tango on a tightrope, but you're not dancing wearing those 'made for the tightrope' shoes on, and there's no net underneath you if you fall.

"Everybody tries to do what you two are attempting – build careers, raise a son, and maintain a loving home – and it's like they are dancing on a tightrope with dress shoes or high heels on. It's scary, and if you don't have the right balance, you will fall."

It was as if all the air was sucked out of the room. Clayton and Darlene both felt their faces turn bright red. Only Mrs. Maples continued eating the soup.

"I like you, Clayton. I see in you much of me as a young man. However, I've noticed some things that send up red flags."

His secret was out in the open. *How does Mr. Maples know these things?* Clayton wondered. Clayton was shocked because he had been producing at a high level and didn't think anyone had noticed his building stress.

"I've watched your personal production which is impressive, but I also know that you don't interact much with the sales representatives in your district. Your inability to connect with people under your supervision indicates you do not understand your role as a district manager. My assessment is that you don't understand how to build relationships, mentor those under your leadership and prioritize."

Maples lowered his voice to a whisper and said, "I also see weariness in your eyes. You are tired and depressed. You may fake your way through another month or two but trust me when I say your fatigue will eventually take its toll.

"Clayton, I consider myself a good judge of people, and I believe you have the gifts and talents that could propel you to success – real success."

Clayton was flattered until Maples continued his line of thinking in a soft deliberate voice, "Yet, if you don't learn to live a balanced life, the dream you have will never happen, and you will find yourself in a life that you will one day loathe. This unbalanced life will never give you what you want. It will destroy you and your family. Do you understand what I'm trying to say?"

Clayton understood perfectly. There would be no promotion.

Maples continued, "Clayton and Darlene, I want to help you both. I want to know if you are willing to meet four friends of mine. These four individuals have a thing or two to say about balance. They each understand an individual secret or principle necessary for a balanced life."

Clayton spoke up and said, "Mr. Maples, I will do anything to learn the things you feel I need to know."

Maples then explained how he would give Clayton two envelopes at work on Monday. Each envelope would contain a name and an address of a friend or former work associate of Mr. Maples. Clayton would assign one name to Darlene, and he would take the other. He and Darlene must each arrange a meeting with the person whose name he or she had and learn the principle the person would teach them. Afterwards they would talk with each other about the Balance Principles they were learning.

One little caveat: A couple of the people Clayton and Darlene would be seeing did not know that they were supposed to be teaching anything. They would only know that Mr. Maples wanted someone to meet them.

At the end of the month, Maples wanted to meet with Clayton and Darlene again to talk about future plans within the company. One thing was promised: Things could not just stay the same.

The remainder of dinner was served, and though the conversation was light, Clayton's mind was racing. "*Tightrope*

Tango" – what kind of crap is that? Clayton steamed. *I thought Maples was sharp. I just want to get out of here and go home.*

As they returned to the car and backed out of the Maples' driveway, Clayton and Darlene began thinking about the little scavenger hunt they had been assigned. Clayton lit a cigarette. Darlene, who tried not to complain about his smoking on a regular basis, decided that since this had not been a regular night, she would tell him again her thoughts on his habit.

"Clay, I hate when you smoke those things."

"Well," Clayton exploded. "If I didn't have to worry about all the money you're spending, maybe I wouldn't have to smoke these things," he barked.

With those words, the war was on as they drove all the way back to their suburban home. For the next 30 minutes, both said things they would regret tomorrow.

When Clayton arrived at the office on Monday, there were two envelopes sitting on his desk from Mr. Maples. Still stinging from the disappointment of not getting the promotion, Clayton contemplated sending the envelopes back to Maples by way of interoffice mail with a note telling Maples exactly what he could do with them.

Thankfully his brain won the battle with his emotions. He opened the envelopes and inside were two names: Ben Holland, aquarist and local businessperson, and Reverend Rodney Shadinger. Clayton had no idea what an aquarist was, so he decided to call him and find out what this Ben Holland was all about.

Analysis

"The biggest difference between success and failure is a committed heart versus an uncommitted heart. A committed heart looks for solutions but an uncommitted heart looks for an escape."
- IKE REIGHARD

"Perspective gives us the ability to accurately contrast the large with the small, and the important with the less important. Without it we are lost in a world where all ideas, news, and information look the same. We cannot differentiate, we cannot prioritize, and we cannot make good choices."
- JOHN SUNUNU

Many successful people advocate lifetime-learning, and for good reason. Management and business guru Peter Drucker said:

"We live in an economy where knowledge, not buildings and machinery, is the chief resource and where knowledge-workers make up the biggest part of the work force."

As you may well know, Drucker worked with business giant GM, as well as General Electric, Intel, IBM, and more. He pioneered the idea of a "knowledge worker," and discussed in The Practice of Management the need to balance values and goals in order to find business success.

What does all of this have to do with Mr. Maples' challenge?

For starters, it is clear that experience is extremely important. Viewing problems from different perspectives can help any successful business person to accumulate experience that can be applied to a whole array of situations and quandaries in the future.

However, when we dig deeper, there is another principle here that is equally important: the ability to learn.

Consider these wise words, this time from psychologist Albert Bandura:

"Learning would be exceedingly laborious, not to mention hazardous, if people had to rely solely on the effects of their own actions to inform them what to do. Fortunately, most human behavior is learned observationally through modeling: from observing others one forms an idea of how new behaviors are performed, and on later occasions this coded information serves as a guide for action."

This quote, from Bandura's book Social Learning Theory, discusses the process of learning, specifically that learning does not come from oneself. Observation is important, as is the application of learned principles.

Learning may seem intuitive, but there are certain ways to learn that may be more effective than others. It is important to discover your own learning style and to prime yourself to learn; in other words, it isn't enough to have the desire to learn or to recognize the importance of learning.

Put yourself in Clayton's situation for a moment. You have no idea what you're supposed to learn, but you have the feeling that it's very important. How do you go about breaking down the situation so that you can get the most returns?

Here is a simple procedure that will help you organize your thoughts:

Step 1 – Prime yourself for learning. To do this, open yourself to the possibility that you can discover a new technique or tool from the upcoming situation. Try answering the following questions:

1. Think about a situation that you found intellectually rewarding, or a situation where you learned something useful. What helped you learn in that situation?

    _____

    _____

    _____

    _____

    a) What external circumstances helped that situation? (e.g. The teacher was inspirational).

       _____

       _____

       _____

       _____

    b) What internal circumstances helped that situation? (e.g. You were interested in the subject.)

       _____

       _____

       _____

       _____

    c) Think of a situation where you did not learn anything. How could you have improved that situation?

       _____

       _____

       _____

       _____

d) Do you have any pet peeves or preconceived notions that prevent you from concentrating in a situation?

_____

_____

_____

_____

Step 2 – Prepare for learning. "Learning opportunities" are not always cut and dried; however, you can prepare yourself to learn in any situation. Imagine attending a poorly organized conference filled with unnecessary presentations and unhelpful speakers. As painful as that sounds, you can still learn something – such as what not to do in your own presentations or when organizing company-wide meetings.

It's alright if the solutions don't appear to you out of the blue; often, it takes time before the answer makes itself clear.

Answer the following questions:

a) What are some traits you admire?

_____

_____

_____

_____

b) Why do some people have these traits and other people do not?

_____

_____

_____

_____

c) Imagine you are talking to someone who works in a completely unrelated field. What are some questions you can ask them to better understand their work?

_____

_____

_____

_____

Step 3 – Observe and review. When you are in a situation where you don't understand something, don't just offhandedly dismiss it. Try comparing the situation to your own. Ask questions, starting with basic ones such as what, how, and why. If there is some problem or issue at hand that is the origin of this situation, examine it closely.

Let's take a look at how this would work with Clayton's dilemma. Mr. Maples feels that Clayton has a problem juggling priorities in his life. He suggests a visit to the aquarist would benefit his young employee. If Clayton were an attentive student, he would consider the following:

- Mr. Maples feels that Clayton has a problem juggling priorities in his life.

- He suggests Clayton visit the aquarist.

- Ask questions: Why an aquarist? What does an aquarist do? How could this be related to the problem?

- Prime himself by opening up to the possibility of learning something. Acknowledge that Mr. Maples' observations may have some merit.

- Prepare himself by asking why some people have their lives together and others don't. Determine some successful traits that he will look for when he talks to the aquarist.

- Observe during the meeting and compare differences in circumstance, personality, attitude, etc. Review after the meeting and determine if there are any traits that he can learn from the aquarist. Check to see if any of these traits can solve the initial problem.

Big Rocks First

When Clayton stopped his car, he was in the driveway of Benjamin Holland, aquarist. Before his meeting, Clayton had done a little research and learned that an aquarist makes aquariums. Most people do this type of work just as a hobby. Ben Holland, Clayton discovered, designed aquariums for some of the richest people in the Chicagoland area.

As they were introducing themselves, Ben said, "I've no idea why Fred C. would want us to meet. I installed his aquarium about seven years ago. We've spoken a few times over the last few years, and since he is such a good man I told him I'd spend a little time with you.

"You can ask me whatever you'd like and I'll do my best to answer. We can sit here and talk for 15-20 minutes, or you can ride with me to my next installation."

Clayton opted for talking to Ben while watching him work, so he helped Ben load the truck. They headed to NFL great Brian Urlacher's house in Schaumburg, a small town just west of the city.

Drawing on his love for sports, Clayton tried to strike up a conversation with Ben by discussing Urlacher's career as it compared to another Chicago gridiron giant, Dick Butkus, but Ben was not interested in small talk.

Clayton learned quickly that Big Ben Holland, who stood 6'7" tall, was a man of few words who took his work seriously. Clayton thought, *It will be a miracle for me to get anything worthwhile out of this guy.*

Ben did say that Brian would not be home because it was the off season for him. Ben's job today would be to get the tank totally set up. The fish would be added later when Brian returned to Chicago.

When they arrived at their destination, Ben pointed to several huge rocks that were on the back of his truck. "Bring those in for me," he grunted as he walked towards the front door.

Clayton made several trips to take all the big rocks into the living room where Ben was busy setting up the huge aquarium that had been delivered earlier. Ben then asked Clayton to bring the other items off the truck.

The other items consisted of many live large and small plants, some ceramic objects, and artificial items like stones, corals, coral skeletons, shells, logs, and plants.

Ben said, "I have no idea what Fred C. wants you to learn, but you just watch real close and maybe something will make sense to you."

Clayton commented that this glass aquarium was a little smaller than the aquarium at Maples' home. Ben didn't answer but studied intently the materials he would use to fully set the aquarium.

After several minutes of thought, Ben went to work. He spent the first couple of hours painstakingly placing the big rocks in the aquarium. Once he was satisfied, he began to move quickly, placing the other items he had brought.

When the tank was completed, water mixed with a special salt was poured into it, and it was beautiful though there weren't any fish.

What am I supposed to be learning from this little excursion? Clayton thought frantically. *This seems stupid. Does Mr. Maples want me to go into the aquarium business?*

"Let me ask you something, Ben." Clayton decided he would use a more direct approach rather than trying to figure it out with no help volunteered from the other party. "What makes this aquarium look so impressive? You have taken a truck load of stuff, and you have blended it in a way that makes sense. People pay you top dollar for what you know how to do. What's your secret?"

Ben took his ball cap off and scratched his head. "I've been building aquariums for a long time. With each aquarium, I want to achieve a feeling of balance. I have tried it different ways, but I think it works best when you put the rocks and big stuff in their places first. I may wrestle with those boulders for a couple of hours, but once they are where they need to be, the rest is a cinch."

As the afternoon progressed, Clayton kept mulling over in his mind what Ben had told him. *To get a feeling of balance the big rocks go in first. That's it!* Clayton thought. *I don't understand it, but I know he just told me the first secret Fred C. wants me to learn.*

As the day wound to a close, Clayton thanked Ben for his time and his insight, helped him pack the truck, then he rode with him back to his car.

Clayton could not wait to talk to Darlene. She had called Reverend Shadinger and was meeting him later in the week, but Clayton had handled his first leg of the journey. He knew this principle was **BIG ROCKS GET PLACED FIRST**. How he and Darlene were going to apply the principle was unknown to him, but he drove to his house thinking maybe Mr. Maples' idea was going to work out after all.

Analysis

"Decide what your priorities are and how much time you'll spend on them. If you don't, someone else will."

- Harvey Mackay

It might seem self-evident that laying down a solid foundation is the first step to developing any kind of functional system. However, what is often neglected is a return to that foundation.

A foundation, in this context, refers to the top priorities in any given situation. These are the important things that help you develop a successful career or personal relationship.

To take a look at why a foundation is important, consider A.M. Monadjem's series, Seven Successes of Smarter Teams. This series breaks down the fundamentals of lucrative businesses. To start with, consider this quote from the first book:

"Teams often create lofty visions, missions, and values that they then stick on a wall. Often, they remain theoretical and isolated without the team realizing that they can be really incredible and useful anchors of day-to-day success."

What this quote is saying is that the foundation – the basic building blocks that outline why a business exists in the first place – can have everyday applications. How is this possible?

For the answer to that question, we turn to the word focus.

Returning to your foundation can provide focus and meaning to both your work and personal life. It helps you trim the excess from your workflow so you're not expending valuable resources on things that are not urgent or even important.

The first step is to answer the question:

What is important to you?

_____

_____

_____

You can answer this question concerning your personal life or your mission statement at work. An example might be, "Developing close personal relationships," or, "Managing a successful B2B (Business to Business) campaign."

Next, the all-important question:

Why is it important to you?

_____

_____

_____

You might wonder why answering this question is important. For that, we'll turn to the idea of Simon Sinek's book, Start with Why: How Great Leaders Inspire Everyone to Take Action. Sinek introduces the idea of the "golden circle" in a lecture, explaining:

"People don't buy what you do; they buy why you do it, and what you do simply serves as the proof of what you believe."

Simply put, Sinek's golden circle states that you first start with why you're doing something; then you proceed to how; and then finally what. We are convinced by why someone is doing something; not simply by what they do or how they do it.

By utilizing the golden circle, you get back to the fundamentals, the reason why any of this is happening to begin with. It helps you make the right decision and creates a cohesive view of every step thereafter.

How can you apply this in everyday life?

Consider revisiting your foundations at work. Maybe you find yourself bogged down with busywork – is that really what you want to be doing? Are you ignoring important tasks that would move the company ahead because of a failure to budget time appropriately? Is there anything that you have forgotten about, perhaps some career goal that you haven't had time to think about in a long time?

You can also apply this in your personal life. Maybe things have been rocky with your spouse – is there any reason for that? What are the things that you really enjoy about your relationship? Are your family relationships still a priority in your life?

Once you revisit your original priorities, you can shift your focus and allocate the necessary resources to course-correct.

What are the priorities that make up your foundation?

Priorities	Why?

Choosing Rocks

At the James' house, there was nonstop speculation about what "putting the big rocks in first" could mean. Clayton thought it meant they needed to decide what was most important to them and to prioritize those things above all others.

Darlene agreed and shared her observation about the last few years together. "I've felt like we have tried to please everybody all the time. It's as if we don't have a road that we, Clayton and Darlene, are on, but rather jump to do any and everything that comes along regardless of whether it fits into our 'aquarium' or not."

Clayton was not sure he understood her and asked for some specifics.

Darlene said, "Remember a week or two ago when you wanted to go to Eddie's little league game, but Travis from next door asked you if you could help him hang the sheetrock in his garage? Remember how you hated saying no to Travis, so you just missed Eddie's game instead? You told me you felt sick about missing his game.

"If you'd thought about it, I know you would have said your family is a big, big rock, and you would need to place that one before you placed the neighbor's rock. I know you love Eddie. I just think perhaps this is one of the things Fred C. wants us to figure out."

"You're so right! And how about this one?" Clayton blurted out. "Can I tell you something I have never told anyone before? I am a pathetic manager at work. I know my district always finishes strong based on my own sales production, but if the truth were known, I don't lead my people, I ignore them."

"Here's the truth about me. I avoid doing the most important things I should be doing as a manager. I do so many things that Sandy could, should, and would do for me. It's not her fault. I fill my day planner with the little jobs to give me something to do so I don't have to build relationships and help mentor my team. If I put my priorities in the right order at work, I believe I would be on my way to living the balanced life Maples feels I should live."

Clayton and Darlene talked late into the night and made decisions about what would be the "big rocks" in their lives. They decided that their faith, which had been ignored for ten years, and their family would be the two huge boulders that would anchor the rest of their lives.

Clayton then went through his job description and looked at the big rocks he had been avoiding. Clayton made some promises to himself and Darlene, and before he went to bed, he changed his day planner to reflect his new commitments.

Analysis

"Action expresses priorities."

- MAHATMA GANDHI

Now that you have made a list of your priorities, it's time to decide what comes first. Number the priorities you listed before and decide what is most important to you above all else.

Brainstorming is nothing without application, so the next step is to analyze how much time you are actually spending on each priority.

Take a look at the circle below. This will be your time management pie chart. Divide it up into sections according to what you spend your time on every month. Some suggested sections include: family, work, hobbies, friends, errands, and personal time.

TIME MANAGEMENT PIE CHART

This is effectively your budget for time. If you can't be sure just how much time you are spending on the different areas of your life, consider starting a journal to keep track of each week. You may be surprised at some of your results!

The next step is to consider whether or not your priorities match up with how you are spending your time (i.e. your "time expenditure"). Take the numbered priorities from before and compare them with your sections from the pie chart, ordering the items from the pie chart from most time spent to least time spent.

How does your list of priorities look when compared to your list of actual time expenditure?

Priorities	Pie Chart

How do the two lists compare? If they are more or less the same, then you're on the right track. If they are askew, then it may be time to reconsider how you are using your time.

Emotional Fuel Tank

On Wednesday, Darlene left work an hour early so she could meet with Reverend Rodney Shadinger, the senior minister of the Barrington Christ Church, the church where Fred C. and True Love belonged. He had given her the first open hour on his calendar, which happened to be from 5:00 PM until 6:00 PM.

He graciously explained he would have to keep the appointment within the scheduled time because he had to lead a congregational Bible study at 7:00 PM. In setting her appointment, Darlene had mentioned that Fred C. Maples had given she and Clayton the reverend's name and had told them that there was a principle they would learn from him.

After being seated, Darlene apologized for the strangeness of the request to come and pick his brain about something Fred C. wanted them to learn.

"It's quite all right. I love Fred C. like I love my own father." Reverend Shadinger beamed, "I am happy to serve you in any way I can."

The warmth of his voice immediately put Darlene at ease. This surprised her. Neither she nor Clayton had been in church very much since their marriage, except for the occasional weekend when his mother and father came to town for a visit.

"Thank you," she said. "I know your time is valuable."

"It won't take long. I know exactly what Fred C. wants you to get from me."

"I am all ears," Darlene replied, and Reverend Shadinger continued.

"I've served as the pastor of this church for 15 years. The first ten years I was here, we experienced numerical growth and expansion unlike anything I'd ever known. I was seeing our membership expand, and I was living in an adrenaline-induced blur.

"I was writing two new talks to give to the congregation each week. I was visiting the sick and homebound and marrying and burying people every week. It was quite a rush. I was flying higher than I'd ever flown and the trip was quite exhilarating.

"One day something changed. I felt fatigued. Not the ordinary, run-of-the-mill fatigue, but a tiredness that felt darker and deeper than I had ever known. I tried to shake it off, but it wouldn't leave me."

Reverend Shadinger took his glasses off and looked as if he were searching for the perfect words to complete his story. "One day, I had just finished preparation for a sermon I would be giving to a couple of thousand church members the next day. I had gotten up from my desk and was about to put on my robe for a wedding ceremony that I was about to perform in our chapel. As I put the robe on my shoulders I was suddenly overcome with tears. I literally sat at my desk and wept for what seemed like an hour."

Darlene was stunned at the story Reverend Shadinger was telling.

He continued, "I had cried before, but not like this. This time I seemed to be crying for no reason. I was succeeding at my job. I felt closer to God than I had ever felt before. I was happy for the success I had known. My family life was exemplary. I had no complaints there. So what was the matter with me? I cleaned myself up and did my perfunctory duties at the wedding, but I knew I needed help and I needed help right away. I searched around and I found a counselor and went to see him."

Darlene interrupted. "Isn't that a little odd for a minister to go to another counselor for help? Aren't you the one who is supposed to be helping others?"

"You hit on part of my problem," Reverend Shadinger said. "I had always thought myself invincible. I learned this was not the case, and counselors, good ones, can be very helpful. However, going to a therapist is not the big lesson I think Fred C. wants you and your husband to learn. I went for several sessions and slowly discovered something that has helped me live the balanced life I have always wanted to live."

Darlene's ears perked up. There was that word: *balance*. This was the big lesson they were to learn here.

The Reverend continued. "Let me say it like this. I have always seen myself with two gauges on the dashboard of life. The gauges were labeled SPIRITUAL TANK and PHYSICAL TANK. I intuitively understood I needed to watch those gauges carefully if I was going to run the race God had called me to run, and quite frankly, I did a good job watching my spiritual life and making sure I didn't cut corners there. I also tried to take care of my physical fitness by eating healthy things and exercising five days a week.

"Here's where I was totally uninformed. My counselor told me there was a third gauge on the dashboard labeled EMOTIONAL TANK.

"You see, in my busy 'successful-looking' life, I had ignored activities and people who filled up my emotional tank. I was almost never at an event where I could just be Rodney. I was always the pastor, leader, prayer, healer, counselor, forgiver, and, pardon my language, spiritual guru. Understand all of these jobs are a part of my calling. I celebrate getting to do these things, but I had to look at my life and honestly admit that I was doing nothing to refill my own emotional tank." Reverend Rodney smiled.

"I never took a vacation just to refuel 'me.' On top of that, I was not spending any time with friends who could help replenish me."

Darlene interrupted again. "How do you know if a relationship is a replenishing one?"

"Great question," Reverend Rodney replied. "You know those dinner parties you and your husband have to go to where you are looking at your watch five minutes after you arrive?"

Darlene laughed. "We've been to a few hundred of those it seems," she said.

"Those would be necessary events that hold little replenishing potential. Now do you remember when you and your husband went out with true friends and the hours sailed by? Neither of you wanted the night to end because it was so exhilarating to be around those people?"

Again Darlene responded, "It's been a long time, but, yes, I do."

Reverend Shadinger said, "Those nights and those friends are the replenishing events and relationships that I was desperate for. This was a scheduling error on my part. I'd simply failed to schedule them into my life.

"To tell you the truth, had I not figured out this aspect of my life, I would have seen everything important to me destroyed. It's crazy now, but I really thought if I ever did anything to refuel myself, I was being self-centered or unspiritual. I have learned that God made me an emotional being, and he expects me to do activities and spend time with people who can help replenish my emotional tank. Do you understand?"

Darlene did. She blinked back some tears welling up in her eyes and thanked the Reverend for his time. She was eager to get back to her home and tell Clayton what she had learned.

Analysis

"Getting in touch with your true self must be your first priority."
- TOM HOPKINS

Though in the previous sections we've been talking about focusing on priorities and allocating resources, Darlene's experience brings balance back into the picture. Maybe all your friends call you the go-to guy or all your coworkers call you Superwoman, but it's crucial to get some downtime in there as well.

If you're worried that downtime will negatively affect your career, just look at Google Labs. Famously, Google has a policy where engineers can spend 20% of their time working on their own projects. This is, effectively, a "working downtime." Instead of asking its employees to burn themselves out on company-wide projects, Google gives everyone some breathing room. Employees can pursue their own interests in a no-stress environment. The result? Google News, Google Maps, and more.

For another example, take a look at the auditing giant KPMG. By allowing employees to have flexible schedules, KPMG is cutting costs and increasing productivity. Because employees can now spend time doing what's important to them – often it is focusing on family and children – they can concentrate fully on their work when they're doing it.

The keyword here is efficiency – doing more in less time. Living a balanced life and getting the kind of rest you need makes it possible for you to have an efficient workflow. By providing your body and mind with the rest needed, you will be able to put 100% into all facets of your life without worrying about diminishing returns.

Not everyone is fortunate enough to work at a company that allows flexible scheduling, but there are still ways you can give yourself downtime. Here are just a few.

PERSONAL TIME – It's important to take a breather every so often. Set aside a period of time where you can do something just for you. If you prefer to be alone, turn off your phone and gently tell your family that you need this time to just be by yourself.

BREATHE – Even if you're not a spiritual person, meditation can be a great way to clear your mind and gain needed perspective on your family life or hectic career. Take some time to just sit and contemplate, maybe on your lunch break or right before bed. Think positively and appreciate all the good things you have in your life. Consciously slow down your breathing. When you relax your body, your mind will relax along with it.

EXERCISE – You don't need to sign up for a yoga class or suddenly become a marathon runner to enjoy the benefits of exercise. Simply stretching or taking a walk can center you and help your body relax.

FRIENDS AND FAMILY – Scientists have found that just smiling and laughing can help lower stress. Spend time with your significant other. Find a time when you can relax together and not talk about work. Re-establish personal connections and rediscover hobbies that you've been neglecting, or find a new hobby that you can enjoy together.

What kinds of things can you do to relax and restore balance in your life?

Activity	Schedule

Checking the Gauges

When Clayton arrived home from work, Darlene was ready to talk about her visit with the Reverend. She began retelling the pastor's story seemingly without taking a breath. When she finished, she paused, cleared her throat, and then said quietly, "Clayton, I've wanted to say this to you for a long time, but I didn't have the words."

She was crying softly and Clayton pulled her close to him.

"What is it, baby?" he whispered.

"When we were first married, we had friends. We hung out with other couples. We cooked out. We played charades and laughed until we almost wet our pants. Honey, since you and I have gotten on the 'fast track' with our jobs, we don't have time to be with the people we enjoy being with anymore.

"I know we have social business responsibilities. I know we also are making some really good friends at our jobs. That's not what I am talking about. I just know we need to schedule some time where we just laugh and play and don't think about being Mr. District Sales Manager or Mrs. Speech Therapist."

"You're right," Clayton concurred. "What kind of life would we really have if we were successful in our careers and empty when it comes to spending time with people we genuinely enjoy spending time with?

"Let me ask you," he wondered. "What puts the bounce back into your step? What's an emotionally replenishing activity to you?"

Darlene smiled sheepishly. "Do you remember when we used to vacation at Uncle Jay's house at Charleston Beach? We'd have the house to ourselves. Every morning we'd wake up and go down to the beach, just you and me. We'd take some sandwiches, a few jugs of water, and the radio, and we'd lie around all day, talking and dreaming about our future. Every hour or two, we'd play in the water or take a long walk to the pier. I loved those days. Those times really filled me up. What about you?"

Clayton thought for a moment and answered, "I loved those times when we could take our watches off, turn our cell phones off, and live a few days uninterrupted. I can't remember the last time we were able to do that. What's crazy is this: it really doesn't matter to me if we are at your parents' or my parents' homes, or if we are sightseeing in Des Moines. If my cell phone is off and my watch is off my wrist, and I am with you, that's all I want."

Darlene chimed in, "Well, I don't want you to disappoint Mr. Maples, so I suggest every few months you start scheduling regular times like that with your wonderful, intelligent and attractive wife."

Laughing at her own silliness, Darlene gushed, "And I will call Uncle Jay and see when we can get on the list to stay at his house in Charleston. Seriously, Clay, I believe we'll do all of our responsibilities better if we know we have a reward that we'll share together just around the corner."

Analysis

"Spend time with those you love. One of these days you will say either, 'I wish I had,' or, 'I'm glad I did.'"
- Zig Ziglar

"No matter what you've done for yourself or for humanity, if you can't look back on having given love and attention to your own family, what have you really accomplished?"
- Lee Iacocca

We have seen thus far how important it is to be aware of the emotional balance in our lives. Why is this important in a career setting?

The keyword here is emotional intelligence. You may have heard this term in a social context or in terms of cooperating with a business team. However, emotional intelligence is even more important when it comes to excelling in a managerial position.

According to TalentSmart, emotional intelligence "affects how we manage behavior, navigate social complexities, and make personal decisions that achieve positive results." Developing emotional intelligence helps you actualize your goals and aligns your inner desires with your actions. It brings together "self-awareness" and "self-management," while also combining "social awareness" and "relationship management." In other words, you can think of it as a method of implementing a solution.

In the paper, "Emotional Intelligence, Leadership Effectiveness, and Team Outcomes," researchers say that, "In order for [an] organization to gain and maintain a competitive advantage, its increasingly valuable employees must be able to adapt well to changing environments both external and internal."

Does that sound familiar to you? It should! Clayton's situation is a direct result of failing to adapt to his surroundings.

He became complacent with the status quo and didn't take steps to change negative behaviors that were impacting his career and personal life. The same problem befell Darlene, who was also just plugging along in a less-than-optimal situation.

So how can you develop emotional intelligence and apply it to your career life?

For starters, you should keep in mind the three facets of emotional awareness:

1. Social feedback
2. Self-awareness
3. Self-regulation

Here are some questions that can help you with your analysis.

Social feedback

Describe your relationships with people. How do they react to you?

_____

_____

_____

_____

Are there any disagreements or negative situations you often find yourself in?

_____

_____

_____

_____

What are some of the reasons you may find yourself in these situations?

_____

_____

_____

_____

Self-awareness

In the situations you described, what role do you play?

_____

_____

_____

Are there any biases that you tend to fall prey to?

_____

_____

_____

What are your social weaknesses? What situations are you the least comfortable in?

_____

_____

_____

Self-regulation

Are there any behaviors or tendencies that you would like to change?

_____

_____

_____

Remember a career situation that was less than optimal. What went wrong? Is there anything you could have done differently?

_____

_____

_____

_____

How can you be more aware of your surroundings? How can you be more aware of yourself?

_____

_____

_____

_____

Finding the right balance is all a part of emotional intelligence as well. When you're running on empty, you won't be able to commit to social situations and you may make mistakes. The key is to strike a balance in your life by giving yourself time to recharge, and then apply observation and analysis to both you yourself and the people in your life.

If you're still not convinced, consider the role of team leader. What makes an effective team leader?

_____

_____

_____

_____

Researchers have found that the team leader's mood or attitude can affect the team. What kind of emotions and attitudes do you tend to display when you lead a discussion?

_____

_____

_____

_____

Analyze your answers to determine if there are any weaknesses. Do you tend to dismiss ideas you don't agree with? Are you overly negative or prone to displays of anger?

The danger of this isn't losing a popularity contest; by acting rashly and not using emotional intelligence, you risk hampering the creativity of your team. You also risk de-motivating your team members and also positioning yourself as an unreliable leader who isn't a "team player."

"Emotional Intelligence, Leadership Effectiveness, and Team Outcomes" finds that, under the tutelage of an emotionally intelligent and therefore charismatic leader, a team develops a solid team identity. This is important because, "team identity has been shown to increase team effectiveness and performance. It serves to bring people together into a cohesive unity..."

No man is an island, and neither is a leader. Keeping an eye on your emotional gauge is extremely important, and so is carefully managing how you act toward others and yourself. When you find the kind of balance that best benefits you, it will also benefit your career, your personal life, and those around you.

Two More Envelopes

Monday, Clayton left his house earlier than usual, excited about the prospects of two more envelopes from Fred C. He stopped at Waffle Palace, a greasy spoon diner a couple of blocks from work, to order breakfast. Eggs, hash browns, bacon, sausage, and a waffle were on the table in no time. Clayton had become a regular at the diner over the last several months and the waitresses knew exactly what he wanted to eat for breakfast.

Darlene had begun to give him a hard time about his expanding waistline, but it wasn't a big deal to him. He simply told her that he wasn't trying to win a beauty contest. After he finished the last bite of the Hungry Man Special, he smoked a quick cigarette and headed in to his office.

Two envelopes were waiting on him, just like the week before. He hurriedly tore into them and read two names: Victor Morris and Patricia Andrews.

Victor's name seemed vaguely familiar, but he had never heard of Patricia Andrews. He decided he would ask Darlene to go visit with Patricia, and he would tackle Victor.

Analysis

"Your choices today will equal your lifestyle tomorrow."
- Ike Reighard

So far, we've been working on tools that can help you improve your own personal sphere of influence. Now is a good time to switch gears for a moment and discuss the people in your life.

Do you have any mentors or role models in your life? These can be a coworker, a parent, a community leader, a celebrity, or even a fictional character.

_____

_____

_____

_____

Why do you admire these people? If you don't have a role model, simply list traits that you think a good role model would have.

_____

_____

_____

_____

Having a role model or mentor can be extremely helpful. If they are in a similar field, they can help you develop a plan of attack. They can offer advice so you can avoid pitfalls and time-consuming mistakes. They motivate you to improve your approach and to meet your career goals.

Even if your role model isn't in your field, they can still offer a lot to you. A community leader can offer advice to help you reach an optimal work-life balance. A spouse or friend can give you emotional support and offer a new perspective.

There may even be some unsung heroes in your past—people who have taught you the tough lessons you have needed to thrive in life.

Can you think of any people in your life who have had a positive influence on you? How?

_____

_____

_____

_____

More importantly, how can you apply these positive lessons in your own life? For example, perhaps you admire a coworker's patience and tenacity. How does she implement these traits? Does she have any special methods or techniques? Think about ways you can shape your life and follow in these peoples footsteps.

_____

_____

_____

_____

Financial Footpath

Darlene pulled her 325CIC BMW convertible into a gravel driveway three miles off of the state highway and fifty minutes from where she, Clayton, and Eddie lived. *There must be a mistake,* she contemplated. *Why would Mr. Maples send me to a simple house like this?*

Darlene did not consider herself arrogant. However, since she and Clayton had been bringing home bigger paychecks, she had prided herself on always buying the best. She was a long way from the girl who grew up on the wrong side of the tracks in the doublewide.

Sure it drove Clayton crazy. He was always getting mad at something, like the last time she went to the hairdresser. Didn't he know it cost to have her hair done by an expert and not by one of these cutters at a retail salon? And what about the new furniture she had recently bought? There was an image they needed to maintain. It cost money to look successful.

Clayton often asked when they were going to begin to save, and her response was always the same: "Soon." For now, they would buy things she thought were important so that they could look like the affluent people they wanted to be.

Walking toward the front door of the humble house that belonged to Ms. Patricia Andrews, Darlene sighed. *Whatever it is I need to learn here, I hope I learn it quickly.*

A slim woman with salt-and-pepper hair opened the door. She was naturally attractive but had a very sad look deep in her eyes. She had little or no make-up on and was wearing jeans and a sweatshirt. She introduced herself and invited Darlene in to the front room to sit down.

She spoke with a calm voice and said she was glad to get to meet a new friend.

Darlene got straight to the point. "My husband works for this older man named Fred C. Maples, and he wants us to learn some lessons about living a balanced life. He's sent us to a few places already where we are learning principles that are supposed to make us better, more successful people."

Patricia smiled knowingly and said, "Please go on."

Darlene took a deep breath and continued. "I think we have the big things figured out. Last week we learned some things about priorities and keeping our emotional tanks filled. We are supposed to learn two more principles from you and another man, and then we are supposed to be home free. Does any of this make sense to you?"

"Yes, it does, Darlene. It is more familiar to me than you might have imagined."

"What do you mean?" Darlene replied quizzically.

Patricia said this was going to take more than a few minutes so she asked if Darlene wanted some hot tea. Darlene said that would be nice and Patricia was gone for a few minutes before returning with a beautiful tea tray, two exquisite cups, and a tea pitcher that looked like it belonged at Mr. Maples' house, not in this humble home.

"Thanks so much," Darlene said as her tea was being poured. "I'm dying of curiosity. Please tell me your story."

Patricia began. "In 1974, I married my high school sweetheart and we moved to Chicago. My husband, Gary, and I thought we had the world by the tail. Coincidentally, in 1981, my husband went to work for Mr. Fred C. Maples. He started as a sales representative and quickly moved up to a district manager."

Darlene shifted uncomfortably in her chair as Patricia continued.

"We'd never really had much in the way of material things before the promotion, but suddenly we had more money than we had ever seen. We bought a house over near Barrington, and I set out to spend the money just as fast as Gary could make it. Let me be more precise, we both spent money like it was going out of style." She looked away for a second to collect her thoughts.

"Here's where the story is going to get a little spooky, Darlene. In 1985, the one and only Fred C. Maples invited us to a dinner at his house with his precious True Love. Is she still living?"

Darlene nodded, and Patricia went back to her story.

"Fred C. told us he saw something special in us, but he also saw some weaknesses we must address if we were going to have balance and success over the long haul. I remember that night as if it were yesterday." Patricia stared off into space for a moment and then resumed.

"Gary and I went home determined to do whatever was necessary to prove to Mr. Maples that we had what it takes to be on his 'A' Team. He had told us of four critical laws of balance. He gave us material to read that he had written on each law. We did well with the first lessons. We were learning; but then we stalled at the taking care of the finances part of his tutorial."

Darlene, who was normally very cold-natured, found herself unusually flushed and beginning to perspire.

"Gary and I were both impulsive, and we both thought we could catch up on savings and living with a margin later. Boy, we were fools." Her voice trailed off as a tear formed in the corner of her eye and coursed down her cheek.

"I remember buying things that were so unnecessary. It was as if there was emptiness in us that we thought could be filled by having more stuff. Well, Mr. Maples saw what was going on, and he did not give Gary the raise he was so dependent on. That little setback made us a little more reckless with our money. You can imagine what it was like. We had credit cards and we ran them up like there was no tomorrow. One day, there wasn't."

"What do you mean?" Darlene whispered.

"We had never seen any real volatility in Gary's job. Back then, it had been a pretty impressive run of higher commission checks every year, but on October 19, 1987 – Black Monday, some call it – the bottom fell out for us.

"The stock market had a historic hiccup that day; investors started pulling out their money in record droves. Looking back, it wasn't nearly as big a deal as the crash of 1929 or the crash of 2009, but for a young couple leveraged to the max, it put us over the edge."

"How badly did it affect you?" Darlene stammered, almost afraid to hear the answer.

"Well," Patricia continued, "our income checks were lower than they had been before, and suddenly, creditors were calling us because we were behind on our bills.

"Understand this was a new experience for Gary and me, and we did not handle it well. We fought constantly about our poor financial decisions – Gary blaming me and me blaming him for the mess we were in.

"In April of 1988, my wonderful husband, Gary, made a huge mistake. It was called security fraud and Mr. Maples had to fire him. Gary Andrews was not a crook." Her voice broke as she spoke those words.

"He was scared. He was trying to get us back on top with one big deal. However, it all blew up in his face. He didn't come home the night he was let go. He went drinking at a little bar near Wrigley Field.

"After getting drunk to forget the pain he was feeling, I guess, Gary headed toward our house in the suburbs. I had gone to sleep and was startled by the knock on the door at 4:13 in the morning.

"When I opened the door, I was looking into the face of an Illinois Highway Patrol officer who told me that my husband had wrapped his car around a tree and would never be coming home to me again." The tears now flowed freely down her face.

Darlene was crying too as she thought about a young couple with so much promise who lost it all because they could not handle their finances, and she cried because she thought about her life with Clayton. He had tried to tell her, but being haphazard with money had seemed so harmless.

Patricia wiped her eyes and continued. "I was a wreck after Gary's death. I hated Mr. Maples. I hated myself and I hated Gary for leaving me in such a mess. I lost our house and all the stuff I thought was so important. Fred C. bought me this house. I accepted it; but I told him I did not want to see or talk to him anymore. I was in deep depression for four or five years."

"How did you survive?" Darlene wondered softly.

"It was tough. After a few years, I gradually began to come out of my despair. I got me a little job at the nursing home about

10 minutes from here, and I have slowly been coming back to life. Over the last couple of years, Mr. Maples has asked me a few times to meet with folks from the office, and I have always felt I was doing a good thing by telling them our story.

"The thing is I remember Mr. Maples' lessons as if they were given to me yesterday. He told us about things like margin and that we should take every pay raise and live on half of the increase and save the rest. He said it was the way he had accumulated his wealth. We were too young or too dumb to listen. Maybe by telling my story to young people like you, it will help some families avoid the pain Gary and I knew."

Darlene interrupted, "Can I ask you something?"

Patricia nodded.

"The tea server you used for our tea. It seems really special. Is there any significance to it?"

"I'm glad you noticed," Patricia said. "This was the last gift Gary bought me. He paid way more than necessary for the tea server, but he thought having it would make me happy. When I lost everything after Gary's death, I was determined to hang on to this. It reminds me that he did really love me and I really loved him. We both just didn't understand there are better ways to show love than mortgaging the future on frivolous things. I hope you understand."

"I do understand," Darlene said and wiped the tears from her eyes one more time.

Patricia and Darlene talked for about thirty minutes more before Darlene said it was time for her to go. They hugged like the friends they both wanted to be and promised they would get together for something social soon.

The fifty minute ride back home was quiet. Darlene never thought about turning on the radio. She and Clayton would be different. They would learn the lessons Mr. Maples wanted them to understand.

Why had she been so foolish with money? When Clayton had wanted to start a college fund for Eddie, she had said it wasn't a good time. They needed to move into the larger house in the more prestigious neighborhood.

When Clayton had talked about trying to save a portion of their ever-increasing raises, Darlene had balked. She felt like every penny should be spent until their family income reached a level that would allow them to live comfortably in the way they wanted to live. Then they could talk about saving.

Now she felt like her actions had threatened her husband and child in ways she had never imagined. She would apologize to Clayton tonight. She would commit to being as balanced in money management as a partner could be. They would not lose their dream. She would not continue making the mistakes she had been making. Clayton would see.

Analysis

Managing money is one of those things everyone knows they should be doing – but most don't do it. The reasons for this disconnect are many. For some, it is a lack of education that keeps them from coming up with an effective plan. For others, it is the discipline necessary to create and then follow a budget. For others it is a dysfunctional understanding of spending as it relates to self-esteem.

Think of the saying, "Time is money"? In the previous sections, we have discussed managing your time. Now we will talk about managing your money.

On the previous pages, you saw an extreme case of what can happen when someone is financially irresponsible. This might seem far-fetched to you, but mishandling money causes people to miss opportunities that could lead to great rewards, or even result in economic disaster. The consequences often are hidden from the view of outsiders. Whether the monetary wreckage is private or public, the devastation is still the same.

Financial irresponsibility weighs heavily on personal relationships. Many divorces occur because of money troubles, particularly within the first two years of a marriage. Weddings are expensive, honeymoons are expensive, and raising a family is expensive. In fact, every new chapter of your life will require money, whether it's having children or moving to a new city to start a job.

Are there any situations where you wanted or needed something but couldn't afford it? Was this because of poor budgeting?

So how can you better manage your budget? You will discover many of the principles used to manage your time are also applicable to managing your financial resources.

In any given month, what do you spend your income on?

Ex. Eating out, cooking, socialization	Percentage of income

Looking at the list above, number your expenditures in order of priority. Naturally some items are essential – for example, housing and food. We'll discuss these in a bit, but for now, consider whether or not you are spending money proportionately. What are the necessities of your life? Do you find that you are going out to eat too often when you could be cooking at home?

There are certain tools, such as Mint.com, that can help you keep track of these expenditures. Always ask yourself if the expenditures are really necessary.

Next, consider this question: Where do you see yourself in five years? In ten?

_____

_____

_____

_____

How much should you save to help you meet these goals?

_____

_____

_____

_____

_____

_____

Saving money can be a hassle if you have to think about it. Many banks, as you know, enable you to set up a savings account and schedule automatic transfers. Consider taking advantage of these services. Many best-selling books on money management have made the case for making automatic money transfers from your payroll check into your savings account. When it is set up to happen automatically, you end up benefiting.

Saving money is much more than just a passive activity, it's also a lifestyle choice, one that can benefit you greatly in both the short and the long-term. Once you become more financially responsible, you won't have to worry about whether or not you can afford that special event that's coming up. You will also be more confident about your future.

Consider the following tips:

1. Set a percentage of your income aside every month and give it to some charitable endeavor you believe in like your church or synagogue, a food kitchen for the poor, an organization that helps children around the world, etc. Doing this as a first priority is a good way to acknowledge your gratitude for having the health to work and make an income. It also has a way of breaking the tendency in all of us toward selfishness. It is counter intuitive, but is a strategy employed by many of the most successful, balanced, and healthy people you will ever meet.

2. Set a percentage of your income aside every month and put it into long term savings. Please notice we have not said a word yet about paying bills. We will get there in a moment, but for now trust us. It is critical for you to give away some money to help people less fortunate than you are, and then you must pay yourself before any bills are paid. This will be imperative to your financial success. Your wealth will not be built by accident. It is not what you earn that will determine the success of your financial future; it is what you learn to keep. This long range savings should be in a place that earns for you a good rate of return. You also should consult with a tax expert to make sure you are getting the maximum benefit for this long range investment.

3. The next step is to learn how to live on less than what you have left. That sounds so easy, but many people struggle with having huge 'wants' and no patience. It is the reason many middle income Americans have a hefty balance on credit cards and virtually no money in the bank. It is the reason many high earning Americans are drowning in credit debt. Learning to live on less than what you make is a critical component to your financial

success. One way to help you learn to live within your means is to create a budget. In this budget you will need monthly expenses like your mortgage payment, utilities, gas for your vehicles, insurance, food, etc. You will also need to include things like monthly contributions to children's college funds, vacation accounts, Christmas and birthday presents and anything else you spend money on. This part of the process seems overwhelming to many but it will make your life better when you see exactly where your money is going, and you force yourself to live within your means.

4. Another critical step is to quickly save enough money to equal 3 months of your income in an Emergency Fund. This money will be what you will use for a medical emergency, or when a major repair is needed on your home or a vehicle. It is hard to imagine how much peace of mind you will have when you have 3 months of income saved in an account you can get to in a hurry when you need it.

5. Another important practice to consider is when you get an increase in your income, don't figure out how you can spend all of the increase. Take half of the new money you will be making and put it into your savings portfolio. You will still have additional money to add to your budget. Doing it this way will take some resolve but it will be worth it as you see your net worth grow.

6. Finally make sure you budget for things that are fun and emotionally replenishing. Don't be a miser. Learn to be generous and learn how to have fun with some of the money you have earned. Just be careful.

These are just a few tips for helping you manage your budget. If you remain self-aware and consider your actions carefully, you will find yourself sleeping a lot easier at night knowing that you are being financially responsible. You will have money invested working for you. You will also have an emergency fund that will help you take care of any sudden medical costs or unexpected vehicle or home repairs. Peace of mind trumps silly purchases made on credit, every time.

Your Body Is a Temple

Clayton followed the address Mr. Maples had given him to a hospice care facility on the outskirts of town.

"This is gonna be good, I'm sure," Clayton said, as he put out his cigarette and stepped out of the car.

After inquiring at the front desk for Victor Morris, Clayton walked down a long hallway to room 24.

When he entered the room, there were five people standing around the bed. Clayton apologized for his interruption, explaining Mr. Maples had given him the address and the name, and he was simply trying to follow up.

The man in the bed laughed and coughed at the same time. Then he spoke in a voice barely above a whisper. "Fred C. told me he was sending a young superstar in to see me. I'm glad you came when you did, son. I'm not sure if you'd-a found me here tomorrow." He laughed and coughed again, but his visitors failed to acknowledge his humor.

Victor looked his guests in the eye and said, "I know this is hard, but I promised an old friend I would talk to this young man. Can you give me fifteen minutes?"

They all nodded and quickly exited the room, leaving Clayton with the dying man.

Victor Morris was a frail, old man. He weighed about 120 pounds. His skin looked ashen, and his muscle tone was nonexistent. He had a little gray hair on the perimeter of his head. His eyes were gray too. He had oxygen attached through a contraption that went in his nose. He looked as if he were 70 years old.

Clayton broke the silence. "I know this is crazy, but Mr. Maples told me I'd learn one of the principles of balance from you. I don't know why I am here nor do I know anything about you. However, I know your situation must be critical."

Victor broke in, "Everybody's situation is critical, kid."

"Right, I understand that," Clayton said, then commented, "I have a vague recollection of a Vic Morris from when I was a kid. He was a catcher with the Cubs in the late 1970's so, he would be a lot younger than you."

Victor smiled and spoke again, "Real good catcher."

"Did you watch him play?" Clayton asked.

Victor tried to smile, but instead he coughed severely. Finally catching his breath, the sick man said, "Don't you get it? He's me."

Clayton was startled at what the old man said. "I am so sorry," Clayton stammered. "I just assumed you would be a much younger man. If my memory serves me correctly you were the Rookie of the Year in '78 when you played for the Cubs. I watched you play those Saturday games of the week on TV. I just had no idea you had made it to the big leagues as an older player."

"Listen, Clayton," the sick man began with impatience in his frail voice. "Maybe you have never seen a man who is about to die, but *surprise*, I am! I am not sixty-five, I am only fifty-three. On a lighter note, I am glad you watched me play."

Clayton saw the strain in Victor's face and realized this was not a joke or a crazy man's journey into dementia. "You really are the ex-major leaguer?"

Victor smiled slightly and began, "I know I don't look like it, but I really am. This is what a guy looks like when his health has gone to hell in a hand basket."

"What happened to you?" Clayton asked softly.

Victor attempted a deep breath and said, "Growing up, I was the strongest, healthiest kid in my neighborhood – good natural athlete, better than average coordination, and bull strong. I thought it'd be like that forever. Anyway, I got drafted by the Cubs after high school and played three years in their minor league system before coming up to the big leagues in 1978. You were right; I was Rookie of the Year. Best year I ever had.

"Met Freddy C. that year, too," Victor continued. "Good guy, that guy. He was already the richest guy in Chicago, and for some reason, he took an interest in some of us players. He had a few of us over to his house to attend some parties. He had a wife named Good Heart or something like that."

Clayton interrupted, "True Love."

"Yeah, True Love. She was something," Victor remembered. "Beautiful and classy — always with Fred. True Love, crazy name, don't you think?"

He coughed again with force to free the congestion in his lungs.

"Anyway, Fred C. used to give me a hard time about my training regimen."

"What do you mean? Did you not work out hard?" Clayton wondered.

"I thought I was invincible. Not only did I not work out, ever, but I did every stupid thing I could do to my body. I abused my body with cigarettes, booze, women, lack of sleep, and later greenies, an amphetamine that kept you up when you had partied too late the night before. "

"After I finished playing, I really let myself go. I ate everything in sight. My weight ballooned up over three hundred pounds."

"I'd see Mr. Maples, and he'd talk to me about my health, but I just laughed at him. Those other guys could eat their salads and drink their distilled water, but not Vic. I was going to go out with Marinara sauce on my fingers and a good beer on my breath." He laughed, but he looked strangely sad.

"When did your health start to fail?" Clayton asked softly.

"In 1995, I lost my first foot to diabetes," Victor said as he pulled back his sheet revealing two thighs but no legs below the kneecaps. "In 1997, I lost the other one. I kept eating garbage I shouldn't eat, and all of it took a huge toll on my kidneys, but none of that compared to the lung cancer I was diagnosed with in 2007."

"I'd smoked a pack or more of cigarettes every day of my life since I was 15. I remember Maples trying to get me to put them down, but I really liked them and didn't think it was really any of his business, to tell you the truth." Victor was talking way more than he should.

When one of the monitors that he was hooked up to started beeping and a buzzer sounded, his nurse came into the room. "Mr. Morris, you're taxing yourself too much. I think you might need to rest a little."

She looked at Clayton, and he nodded.

"Let me talk just a minute more and I'll be done," Victor said. The nurse smiled, winked at Victor, and left the room.

"I was as dumb as a rock," Victor said through clenched teeth as the veins in his forehead expanded, indicating a surge of pain through his body. "Mr. Maples told me my health was a precious gift and that I should 'treat my body like it was a temple' or something like that. Smart guy, that Maples. He's over eighty, and I'm fifty-three; he looks like that fella who played James Bond in the movies and I look like a character from *Night of the Living Dead*."

The door opened and the visitors from earlier walked back into the room. "Dad, you need to rest now for a few minutes," one of the men said as he approached the bed.

Victor raised his hand to his son, looked at Clayton, and said, "You tell Maples I love him and that he was right. I should've taken better care of this body of mine."

Clayton apologized to the guests for the intrusion and walked toward the bed. "Victor, you've told me exactly what I needed to hear. I'll never forget you. I'll be praying for you these next few days. OK?"

"OK," Victor said in a voice that was now barely audible. "Hey, I really was a good catcher."

"I know you were, Victor. You were great. Remember, I watched you play." With that last statement, Clayton bowed his head and walked quickly from the room. He felt a lump in his throat and tears in his eyes as he thought about Victor being only days from his death; *superior athlete dead in his mid fifties.* It seemed so crazy.

As he drove back toward his home, Clayton thought about the message Fred C. wanted him to get. Even though you are not an athlete anymore, your body is still an important part of the balanced life. Treat it with respect. What did Victor say Maples told him? Clayton thought. Oh yeah! 'Your body is a temple.' I get it.

Analysis

"Take care of your body. It's the only place you have to live."
- JIM ROHN

"When you have your health you have hope, and the person with hope has life's greatest treasure."
- IKE REIGHARD

Living the best life possible involves maintaining good health. We have never met a wealthy person in poor health who wouldn't gladly give all of his riches to have his health back.

Health is a very personal topic to talk about, but it's incredibly important. We recognize people are wired differently. Some people have huge appetites while others eat like birds. Some enjoy sweating outside doing yard work while others prefer staying in spaces that are air conditioned. Some people are comfortable in a gym while others are more comfortable at a mall. How you put together your health plan will be based on your unique personality. This chapter deals with the universally accepted principles that are keys for your success.

Please remember before beginning any new fitness regimen to consult a medical doctor to determine your level of general health.

There are 3 components necessary to achieve maximum results with your health. You must learn to eat healthy foods. You must participate in regular physical activity. And you need to eliminate habits that have been proven to take a negative toll on your body such as smoking cigarettes, drinking alcohol excessively, and abusing legal and illegal pharmaceuticals.

The market is flooded with food plans for people who want to take off unwanted fat and begin living a healthier life.

People are different and respond differently to these programs. The main thing to remember is if you want your body to run at its highest capacity, make sure you are giving it the best fuel possible. Lean meats and green vegetables are always a good choice. Unhealthy processed foods will never give you the long term health you desire.

Food is the fuel for your body. Good food choices can provide energy and a sense of well-being. An unhealthy diet can lead to fatigue and poor health.

What food items do you find yourself eating most often?

_____

_____

_____

_____

_____

Are there any changes to your diet that you need to make for better health?

_____

_____

_____

_____

_____

Physical activity is also a requirement. People who exercise regularly are more alert and miss fewer days of work. Now you can see the reasoning for companies that have gyms built into their workplaces! Thirty minutes a day of moderate activity is a huge improvement for most people. Some will want to go further and will see the benefit of adding high intensity training on at least three days a week. There are many good programs available that will give you choices you need to find the best workout plan for you.

Naturally, wanting to improve your health isn't just centered around how successful you are at work, but for those who find it difficult to get off the couch and get on a bike, it can offer an incentive. Even if you don't value your overall health, if career goals are something that are important to you, then you should take note. A study cited in the Huffington Post finds that "…eating unhealthily is linked with 66 percent increased risk of loss of productivity, while rare exercise is linked with a 50 percent increased risk of low productivity. …And smoking is linked with a 28 percent increased risk of loss of productivity."

It makes sense that exercise can help productivity. Consider the fact that your body has a natural rhythm: if you exercise, you tend to sleep better, and if you sleep better, you tend to be more alert during the day. When this process is repeated you are on your way to becoming a much more energetic contributor at work.

It also helps that exercise releases serotonin into your blood stream, relieving stress and elevating mood. There are countless benefits to leading an active life, from your own personal well-being, to your career, to even your budget. If you develop health complications later in life, you'll be paying for them with both your wallet and your body.

So how can you motivate yourself to lead an active life? And what is an active life anyway?

It differs from person to person. Some people find their exercise in dance classes or yoga sessions, and others blow off steam playing basketball or jogging. It doesn't matter what kind of activity you do; what matters is that you do it.

What are some types of physical activity you enjoy doing?

_____

_____

_____

_____

Another key part of being health-conscious is to set a schedule. It may be difficult to set up a routine, but once you have it, you'll find that you enjoy it.

How often will you exercise? Be realistic.

_____

_____

_____

_____

Once you start exercising, you may want to start implementing more healthy decisions in your lifestyle. You'll start drinking more water, for example, and you may consider changing up your diet as well.

Making healthy choices involves both adding good practices and eliminating bad ones. The U.S. Department of Health and Human Services states emphatically in the article The Health Consequences of Smoking: A Report of the Surgeon General: "Smoking harms nearly every organ in the body. Smoking causes many diseases and reduces the health of smokers in general."

Abusing alcohol is another hindrance to walking in health. According to most health care specialists, drinking alcohol in moderation is not detrimental to you. However, when done in excess it can severely affect your health and have serious long term consequences.

And finally you must be careful with your use of medication. Obviously, medicine can have huge life saving benefits. However, abusing medicine is a growing national epidemic.

Leading a healthy life doesn't necessarily have to be complicated. You can begin making healthy food choices today. And you can increase your activity by taking walks during your lunch break at work, or opting to take the stairs instead of the elevator. It's the small things that matter, and if you put your mind to it, you'll be able to find the right fit.

The most important thing to keep in mind is commitment. Once you find your motivation, be it health, career or lifestyle, then commit to doing the appropriate work necessary to see significant results. Remember that planning for the future is incredibly important.

Applying the Lessons

When Darlene arrived at the house, Clayton had already been there about forty-five minutes. He was playing with Eddie as he had tried to do every day since the lesson about priorities he had received from Benjamin Holland. He wanted to practice the principles of balance he was learning from Fred C. and from the interesting people he and Darlene had met.

When Darlene came through the door, it was obvious that she had been crying. Clayton told Eddie to get ready for bed and then went into the living room where Darlene was sitting.

"You okay?" he asked.

"Yeah, how about you?" she said softly.

"I'm good," Clayton said. "I feel like tonight Mr. Maples got a very serious point into my very thick head."

"Me, too," Darlene said, "me, too."

Darlene and Clayton talked until two in the morning about the feelings they both had about what they were learning. They were amazed that two college-educated people could have been so far off track when it came to living a truly balanced life.

Both Darlene and Clayton committed to getting on a good financial plan. They knew if they were ever going to become all they could be, they were going to have to be financially disciplined.

Darlene told Clayton that Patricia Andrews had mentioned a principle Mr. Maples had tried to teach Gary and her about saving one-half of every pay increase. Darlene felt this would help her and Clayton stop spending every penny they received in bonuses or salary increases. Clayton agreed, and they spent a long time talking about other ways they could get on the right track with their personal finances.

As they were finishing the financial discussion, Darlene said, "Clayton, do you understand, I want to be your soul mate. I don't want to be a person who is never content. I want to treasure our friendship, our passion, and our precious son, Eddie, not all the stuff we can buy."

Tears formed in her eyes as she thought about Patricia Andrews and the pain she felt in losing Gary, her husband and best friend.

Clayton pulled her close to him and kissed her softly on the forehead. "I want that, too."

"Let me tell you about what happened to me." Clayton's excitement startled the now relaxed Darlene.

"I'm ready," Darlene responded as she sat upright. "Tell me."

Clayton told Darlene of his conversation with Victor Morris. He told her how he felt as he looked at Victor, knowing he was going to die very soon. He explained how he felt when Victor talked about his habits that led to his health failing.

"Little D," Clayton said affectionately, "I've always admired how disciplined you have been with your eating and workouts. I know your schedule is quite full, yet you always take time to stay in excellent shape. I want you to know I'm very sorry I've not been as diligent as you."

They both laughed.

"OK, I've not been diligent at all," Clayton smiled and continued. "I know that if I'm going to be the man I can and should be, I need to think about being fit. I want to be here for you and Eddie as long as I possibly can. I also want to be a good example for our son. I want him to see a dad who takes care of his health."

After a thoughtful pause, Clayton said, "I promise you from this day forth I'm going to stop putting poisonous things in my body like cigarettes and Waffle Palace cuisine."

Darlene, the former cheerleader, clapped her hands and exclaimed, "Go Clayton, go Clayton, go Clayton."

Seizing the moment, Clayton called for quiet from his one-woman cheering section and said, "From this day forward, I'm going to begin to work out and build muscles."

"Muscles," Darlene squealed and swooned jokingly.

"I'm going to have so much more energy than I have had lately that my wife is going to literally beg me to not be so sexy and amorous."

Darlene gave him her best tiger growl, and they both laughed at how silly they were getting as the night grew later.

Clayton picked up his wife and headed for the bedroom.

As their passion picked up intensity, Clayton whispered to Darlene, "I don't know about you, but for me, this sure beats Waffle Palace."

"Way better," Darlene said.

"Do we have any syrup?" Clayton inquired.

They laughed so hard that they feared they would wake up Eddie.

Analysis

"Treasure the love you receive above all. It will survive long after your gold and good health have vanished."
- OG MANDINO

To recap the principles we've covered thus far:

1. Determine what activities are most important to you and prioritize them.

2. Schedule events that help you emotionally recharge.

3. Develop emotional intelligence in your work and personal life.

4. Consider the role models in your life and how you can learn from them.

5. Manage your budget and plan for the future.

6. Try to be active and lead a healthy lifestyle.

You might be able to see that all of these work in conjunction with one another. Once you determine your priorities and "get back to the basics," the other principles work as tools to help you stay in tune with your foundation.

Taking the time to recharge and relax will make sure that you are in the best mental and physical condition to tackle all the challenges of your life. It also gives you time to think about your goals and how you are currently approaching them. Don't shy away from self-evaluation; it can be your most powerful tool.

Self-evaluation is an ancilary part of the three facets of emotional intelligence we talked about: social feedback, self-awareness, and self-management. Once you have the information from self-evaluation and the feedback from people around you, you can begin to think about how you act and behave in situations. Are there any strengths you should present at work? Are there any weaknesses that you should try to bolster? Emotional intelligence makes you a more well-rounded person, as well as a great leader.

And what great leader doesn't plan for the future? Budgeting your money and taking care of your body are both activities you should pursue with all diligence. They will pave the path toward the future and make it that much more possible for you to reach your goals.

So far in our journey with Clayton and Darlene, we've been watching them learn the principles of leading a balanced life. Now let's see how the rest of the story unfolds as they apply these principles.

Time to Tango

Mr. Maples told Clayton he was very proud of the progress he was seeing in his performance as a district manager and that he should not be discouraged about his failure to get the regional manager job. "Work on the Laws of Balance and your future will be brighter than you can imagine," Mr. Maples said whenever he would pass Clayton at work.

Clayton and Darlene did work on all the things they had learned from Mr. Maples' little challenge. They put the BIG ROCKS in first by prioritizing, with God and their faith being first, the family second, and their careers third.

They began to cultivate friendships with people who "filled up" their emotional tanks. For the first time in a long time, they scheduled evenings that were just for fun – no business stuff allowed. They also booked a week at Uncle Jay's place at Charleston Beach. It was a perfect seven days for Darlene, Clayton, and Eddie. They were feeling emotionally full, and loving every minute of it.

Their finances also were shaping up. It was a process. They bought and devoured a book by Dave Ramsey called *The Total Money Makeover*. The seven principles he taught in the book made sense. Both Darlene and Clayton committed to implementing his plan. Darlene's total transformation did not happen overnight, but slowly she recognized her weakness with credit card spending. She cut them all up and presented them to Clayton one day when he came home from work. They also sat down together, created a budget that was financially sound, and did their best to live within that budget.

In January, Clayton and Darlene received little pay increases. Rather than altering their budget so they could spend more money, they rationally decided to stock away more money into their savings portfolio.

Clayton began to exercise and eat healthier. His efforts showed not only in his appearance but also in his performance at work and in the energy he had when he played with Eddie in the evenings. Clayton was also discovering how good it made him feel to practice discipline in his food choices. It made him walk taller and feel more successful than he had ever felt when he was living on junk food.

The principles were trickling down to Eddie. One day, Clayton came back from the office and Eddie was doing his homework in the family room.

"Come on, tiger," he said. "Let's go throw the baseball around."

"Can't do it, Dad," Eddie replied. "I've got a big test tomorrow and someone really smart told me I need to put the big rocks in first."

Clayton feigned disappointment but was really proud that the whole family was embracing the principles of balance.

Did they find the changes were easy to make? Not at all. It's not easy to alter a lifetime of bad habits. But with each step, they made toward a balanced life, Clayton and Darlene felt healthier than they had ever believed possible. Life for the James family now had balance, rhythm and grace.

Remembering Fred C. Maples' original illustration, Clayton mused, *I think we might be ready for Dancing with the Stars. The Tightrope Tango is an amazing dance once you learn how to do it.*

Analysis

"What lies behind us and what lies before us are small matters compared to what lies within us."

- RALPH WALDO EMERSON

So far, so good. Clayton and Darlene have committed to the changes in their lifestyle. They've learned from Maples' lessons and they are applying these principles to their daily lives.

Take a moment to consider these principles and how they apply to your life. Maybe you've got the budgeting thing down but you never take the time to relax. Maybe things are great, but you still wish you had some kind of mentor to help you along the way. Maybe you wish you spent more time with your spouse, or maybe you've been meaning to get around to that New Year's resolution of hitting the gym.

In the space below, make a list of the principles that your life could benefit from.

_____

_____

_____

_____

_____

_____

Consider what obstacles may get in your way. These can be external (ex. lack of time) or internal (ex. bad track record with following commitments).

_____

_____

_____

_____

_____

_____

_____

_____

What are the ways you can overcome these obstacles? Make concrete statements.

_____

_____

_____

_____

_____

_____

_____

Now it's time for you to commit to change in your life. In the space below, take the time to think about how you can effect these changes. Start each sentence with the words, "I commit to..." Set a deadline if you're feeling particularly confident. You'd be surprised by how putting something down in writing can make it official!

_____

_____

_____

_____

_____

_____

_____

Summertime

The summer was an exciting time for Clayton and Darlene. They enjoyed watching Eddie flourish and become one of the best players on his baseball team. Eddie pitched and played first base on an A level Little League team that was handling the local competition with ease.

On the job front, Clayton believed a regional manager position was going to become available, and he confidently felt that he would be the man for the job.

At work, every week or so, Clayton saw Mr. Maples in the hallway and they would speak. Maples was very encouraging, letting Clayton know if he lived a balanced life, he would know no limits to where he and Darlene and their family could go.

Maples never failed to ask about Darlene and Eddie. He was such a good man and he genuinely seemed to love and care for Clayton's family. Maples even seemed interested in Eddie's exploits on the baseball diamond. His questions about Eddie's team and year always made Clayton feel extremely proud. Clayton made a mental note of this often: *As I grow older, I want to be a man just like Maples.*

Analysis

"Your most effective mentor is the one who brings out the best in you!"

- IKE REIGHARD

Recall that in an earlier section, we addressed the benefits of turning to a mentor or a role model. As you learn new life principles, consider becoming someone else's role model. It's a common concept that teachers learn just as much as students. As we discussed, any situation can be a learning situation if you prime yourself that way.

Is community outreach a possibility for you at this point in your life?

_____

_____

Volunteering and helping others can help you learn more about yourself. It can motivate you to adhere to the principles that are important to you. Tutoring someone may even result in some questions you don't have the answer to, in which case you may, in the course of seeking a solution, learn something new.

What are some things that you are knowledgeable about?

_____

_____

_____

_____

_____

How can you share this knowledge?

_____
_____
_____
_____

You don't have to go as far as volunteering around the community; you could simply resolve to become a role model or mentor to someone in your family. Help the people in your life, you'll be helping yourself as well.

The Promised Promotion

The week was busy like every other week at FC MAPLES. There had been a week-long sales training class for Clayton to present to new securities agents and evaluation meetings with all the people in his district. He had sat down with several big clients and talked about ways to increase their portfolio's profitability.

He also boasted to anyone who would listen about Eddie's big game this weekend. Eddie would be pitching the final game of the Little League Greater Chicago World Series for boys 9-10 years old. Clayton began almost every conversation with coworkers with, "Hey, did I tell you about my amazing son?" They would laugh and then Clayton would do play-by-play highlights of Eddie's year.

Clayton ended his day on Friday by spending about an hour with his assistant, Sandy, going over his schedule for the next few weeks. As he was beginning to pack up his briefcase for the commute home, Mr. Maples knocked on the door and stepped into Clayton's office. Maples spoke with great intention: "I want to meet with you and Darlene about a great advancement I have for you in our company. This is what you two have been working toward for the better part of the last year. Are you excited?"

Clayton was a little dumbfounded at Maples approach; however, he nodded his head vigorously, indicating he was very excited about the prospects of his promotion to regional manager.

Without skipping a beat, Maples said, "Fine, I'm heading home. I will see you and Darlene at my house tomorrow at 3:00 PM. Don't miss this meeting because it will be the most memorable promotion you will ever have."

Once Maples was out the door, Clayton sat in his office, paralyzed at what Maples had just told him. *I have worked a long time for this*, Clayton considered. *I can't believe it's really all coming together.* He put his feet up on his desk and audibly said, "Clayton James, regional manager."

When Clayton walked through the door at home, Darlene was in the kitchen preparing dinner. Clayton came up behind her and kissed her on the neck and whispered in her ear, "You look more beautiful than any regional manager's wife I've ever seen."

Darlene looked into Clayton's eyes incredulously. "What are you talking about?" Darlene demanded, her voice rising in anticipation of Clayton's answer.

"That's right, my dear. You are looking at the new regional manager of FC MAPLES," Clayton said proudly.

Darlene screamed and Eddie joined them in the middle of the kitchen for a James family group hug.

After hugging and giving high five's to his dad, Eddie ran out to play and Clayton continued talking to Darlene. "Mr. Maples wants you and me to be at his house tomorrow at 3:00 PM for him to give me the most memorable promotion I will ever have."

Darlene interrupted, "What time did you say?"

"Three o'clock," Clayton began. "It shouldn't take long. I am guessing a couple of hours at Fred's C.'s house should just about do it."

"Honey," Darlene began, "do you remember what is happening at 3:00 PM tomorrow?"

"Sure," Clayton said. "We are going to Maples' house and – oh no! I totally forgot. The championship game is at 3:00 PM tomorrow. I've already told Maples I'll meet with him. What am I going to do?"

Darlene stated, "Let's not panic. Try to call him and see if we can move the time. I am sure he will understand."

"Are you crazy?" Clayton barked. "You don't blow off a meeting with the CEO of the company."

"I don't think going to our son's championship baseball game is 'blowing off' a meeting," Darlene retorted, sounding more than a little agitated.

"I know," Clayton said. "I didn't mean it that way. Listen, we have done really well on every one of the principles Mr. Maples has wanted us to address. I think this is another thing entirely."

"Here's what needs to happen," he continued, "I think I need to go to the meeting, and you need to go to Eddie's game. I'll hate not being there, but this way both things can take place. I'll go to the meeting with Mr. Maples, and do my best to finish up as quickly as I can so I can meet you at the ballpark. Maybe I can see at least the last inning or two."

Darlene asked, "Clayton, are you sure? Don't you think following through on the commitment you've made to Eddie will be most important?"

"Darlene," Clayton said with a bit of irritation, "I don't think there's anything else we can do about this. Please don't make this any harder. I'll handle this, and Eddie will understand."

Darlene said she understood, but the way she handled the pots and pans as she prepared the dinner told another story. Darlene was not mad at Clayton. She was just very frustrated at the predicament she felt Clayton was in.

Clayton thought things were a little chilly around the house, but believed tomorrow everything was going to work out fine. Not another word was spoken about the scheduling conflict before Clayton and Darlene retired to bed.

Just before they turned the lights out, Darlene cuddled up with Clayton and said, "I'm really proud of all you've accomplished. I know you're doing the right thing. Just remember Eddie has been expecting you to be there cheering him on. Make sure you talk to him and let him know where you'll be during his game. I love you, honey."

Clayton whispered, "I love you, too.

Analysis

"Character is never made in a crisis but it is certainly revealed in a crisis."

- IKE REIGHARD

A common problem is an inability to adapt. It can be difficult to stick with our commitments in the face of adversity. Consider the story above – Clayton and Darlene were doing extremely well, applying all the principles they learned, reconnecting with each other, and excelling in all arenas of their lives. Then a conflict of interest emerged and challenged their commitment.

In your own journey to reach your goals, you will encounter setbacks and obstacles. You may even relapse briefly.

It's important to remember that this is okay. Just brush yourself off, reaffirm your commitment to change, and try once again.

What's important is to remind yourself why you wanted to make the change to begin with. Draw up a revised plan of how you can get back on track. Know what works and what doesn't work for you, and if you're struggling, don't be afraid to ask for help.

In the space below, discuss the reasons why you are committed to leading a balanced life.

_____

_____

_____

_____

_____

_____

_____

_____

Miracles Really Still Happen

Eddie was unusually hyper when he got up on Saturday. Clayton figured it was simply the anxiety of being the starting pitcher in such a big game. Clayton was anxious himself. He had asked himself a thousand times if he was sure he was doing the right thing. This new job would mean more money, and more money would mean more vacation time, and more vacation time would certainly make up for Dad having to miss one game.

Eddie will have other games, he thought. *I need to stay focused and go meet with Mr. Maples.*

At 1:30, Eddie and Darlene were about to head to the ballpark and Clayton had still not told his son he would be missing the game.

Clayton needed to talk to Eddie before he had to leave. He called for his son to join him in the study. "Eddie, I need to tell you something."

Eddie came running and said, "Daddy, I need to tell you something, too."

Clayton said, "OK, kiddo, you go first."

Eddie began, "Daddy, I'm going to pitch really good today."

"I know you are, son," Clayton said.

"And you know what else?" Eddie asked his dad.

"No, you tell me," Clayton said.

Eddie smiled and said, "I really think I'm going to hit a home run today, and when I do, I'll be hitting it just for you."

Eddie had never said anything like that to his dad before. Pitching, not hitting had been Eddie's strength. Clayton had taken him to the peewee batting cages often for practice. Eddie had certainly tried to do what his dad told him to do at the plate, but his lack of confidence always seemed to win out and his hitting was mediocre. Eddie looked up at Clayton and smiled. Clayton felt the weight of his decision stronger than ever before. This was his son. His priority. His passion.

"Daddy, are you going to be cheering for me?" Eddie asked.

Clayton said gently, "Of course I will, Eddie. I wouldn't miss seeing you play in this game for the world." Then he squeezed Eddie tightly.

Darlene had been standing at the door of the study. When her eyes met Clayton's, she mouthed, "Are you sure?"

He nodded his head and mouthed back, "Absolutely."

Clayton knew exactly what he needed to do. "Honey," he called out to Darlene, "will you go on and take Eddie to the field? I need to make a phone call, and then I'll be right behind you."

Darlene grabbed Eddie by the arm and said, "Come on, big boy. I've got to get you to the game."

When Darlene and Eddie were out the door, Clayton began dialing Mr. Maples' phone number. Clayton had only called his boss's number a few times in his career with the company. The previous calls had gone through without a glitch. This was not normal. He called the cell and the house phones. The phones rang but never went to voicemail.

Great, Clayton thought. *No one is answering their phones, and I can't drive to Maples house and then to the game in time because they are sixty miles apart.*

TIGHTROPE TANGO

After dialing both numbers several times with no one answering the phones, Clayton knew he would have to just go to the game and pray Mr. Maples would not be too angry with him. He had resigned himself to the fact that he would not be obtaining the regional manager position. He just hoped Mr. Maples would understand why he had chosen to go to his son's state championship game over meeting with him.

As Clayton drove into the parking lot, Eddie warmed up, craning his neck to find his dad in the stands. *I am doing the right thing. It may cost me the promotion, but that's OK. I'm living a balanced, healthy life, and this is a priority I believe in.*

When Clayton trotted up to the field, the game was just about to begin. Eddie was already on the mound getting ready to start his warm-up pitches. When he saw his dad, he sighed, smiled and gave a big wave to him. Then he fired the ball to his catcher.

Clayton and Darlene watched the game from the fence on the third base side of the field. From this vantage point, they could see the game clearly and say an encouraging word to Eddie when he came to the dugout between innings.

The game was quite exciting, and Eddie was pitching exceptionally well. It was definitely a pitcher's duel because neither team was generating much offense. Eddie's team was down 1-0. The only run came when Eddie's right fielder misjudged a fly ball, and the batter was able to run all the way around the bases for an inside-the-park home run.

Eddie was also swinging the bat well. After three at-bats, he had two singles and a walk.

Clayton and Darlene held hands often during the game. They were excited for Eddie and excited about the life they had built. It really had become a life of balance.

They had a good family, good friends, and good jobs. They both were passionate about work and just as passionate about being together. They budgeted their income better and were making serious provisions for their future. Clayton had gotten back into shape. He was thirty pounds lighter and hadn't smoked a cigarette in almost a year. Life was becoming all it was supposed to be. It really didn't matter too much that Clayton was going to miss this promotion. He knew he brought value to FC MAPLES, and he knew his time would ultimately come for whatever higher-level job Maples thought he could handle.

The game was a nail-biter with neither team able to put any more runs on the board. In the bottom of the last inning, one of Eddie's teammates finally made it to first base. There were two outs, and it was Eddie's turn to bat. *This couldn't be possible, could it?* Clayton reasoned. *This is the reason I was supposed to be here and not at Mr. Maples house. Eddie is going to hit a game-winning home run like in a movie, and as his dad, I need to see him do it.*

Eddie confidently stepped into the batters' box and watched as the pitcher threw a fast ball right down the middle of the plate. The fans for Eddie's team let out a groan while their opponents screamed and cheered with delight.

Eddie looked at his dad leaning on the fence and he seemed to smile. The next pitch came towards home plate and Eddie swung with all of his might. The ball shot off his bat like it had been fired from a rifle. His parents hugged each other tightly, and they watched as the ball went towards the outfield fence.

"Yes, yes, yes," Clayton yelled as the ball soared towards the bleachers beyond the fence. In a moment when time seemed to stand still, the ball cleared the outfield fence just outside of the foul pole.

"Foul ball," the umpire screamed.

Eddie had already rounded first and had to run back to the plate, now with two strikes on him.

Clayton was as nervous for his son as he had ever been before. Two outs, a runner on first base, Eddie hitting with two strikes against him.

"You can do it, big man," Clayton shouted as the pitcher began his windup.

When the pitcher released the ball, it was as if all the fans, probably close to a thousand people, collectively held their breaths. Eddie swung, made contact and the ball headed towards deep left field. Darlene and Clayton jumped into the air and began to cheer: "RUN, RUN, RUN!" The left fielder staggered backwards to the fence, and almost falling down, lifted his glove and made the catch.

"Out three – game over!" The umpire shouted. Eddie's team and fans let out a huge sigh, and the opposition team's parents and fans ran onto the field to celebrate with the victors. Eddie trotted back towards his dugout on the verge of tears.

Darlene felt a little tear in her eye but wiped it away quickly. *I'm so glad Clayton was here*, she thought. *This is definitely a time when a young boy needs his dad.*

Eddie ran into his dugout where his coach hugged him and told him he played a great game. The coach gathered up the equipment and then had the boys run into left field so he could talk to them for a few moments. Clayton and Darlene stood against the fence and strained their ears to hear the things the coach was saying. Clayton heard the coach say to Eddie he had nothing to be ashamed of; he had pitched good enough to win the game, and the last at bat could have just as easily been dropped. Clayton just wanted the coach to hurry up and finish so he could hug his little boy and tell him how unbelievably proud he was of him.

When Eddie finally walked through the gate to where his parents were standing, he looked up at Clayton and said, "I'm sorry. I didn't hit a home run for you, Daddy. I really tried."

"I know you did, son," Clayton said, bending down to give his son a great big hug. "I want you to know I really am proud of you. During your game, I wanted everyone in the whole world to know that Eddie James is my son."

"Listen, Eddie," Clayton continued as he pulled Eddie close to him, "sometimes you can do everything just right, and it doesn't turn out the way you want it to. Do you understand what I'm trying to say to you?"

Eddie nodded his head and said, "Dad, I really did think it was going over the fence. If that long foul ball had stayed fair, we would've won the game." Eddie was beginning to cry just a little.

Clayton looked his son in the eyes and said, "Eddie, I know how you feel." Clayton looked at Darlene, and she smiled at him. "If we know we did our best, that's all we can do."

Eddie's friend, Jeff, from the team called out to him. Eddie left his mom and dad to see what Jeff wanted. After a moment, he returned with a smile on his face.

"Thanks, Dad, for the good talk. Hey, the team is going to Dairy Queen to get ice cream. Do you mind if I ride there with Coach Doug and Jeff?"

"That will be fine. You go on ahead. We'll be there in just a few minutes," Darlene said with a big smile on her face.

"Wow, does he bounce back fast or what?" Clayton exclaimed to Darlene as Eddie ran towards his coach's car.

"That's our boy," she chirped. "You know something else? I am very proud of you, Mr. James."

"Whatever for?" Clayton asked innocently.

"You had a tough decision to make, and it cost you a bunch, but I think in the long run you did the best thing you could do. I want the whole world to know that Clayton James is my husband!" Darlene's voice was now very loud and people were beginning to look their way.

"Shhhhh," Clayton said. "You're embarrassing me."

Just then, over Darlene's shoulder, Clayton saw Mr. Maples walking directly towards them.

As he approached, Clayton stammered, "Mr. Maples, I'm so sorry. I forgot about a scheduling conflict, and I tried to call..."

Mr. Maples cut him off. "Clayton, is this the way you treat your employer?"

"I know it looks bad, and I want you to know I never ever would disrespect you or your position, Mr. Maples." Clayton saw his career quickly sinking before his very eyes.

"Clayton, had you been at my house today, I was fully ready to give you a promotion to regional manager," Maples said.

"I know, sir, and I'm truly sorry," Clayton said.

Maples continued, "But since you were not at my house, and you were here watching your son pitch in this championship baseball game, you are going to have to settle for a promotion to CPO. This is a position I've just created, and I want you to be it."

"I can't tell you how sorry I am," Clayton responded. Then it dawned on him what Maples had said. "Excuse me, what did you say?"

Smiling, Maples said, "Clayton, for a year, I have watched you embrace every good thing about living a balanced life. You have taken to these principles better than any employee I've ever had. And Darlene, you are to be commended as well. I've also watched you grow in balanced living. You are as fine a partner as I've seen since I married my own True Love."

Darlene and Clayton had their arms around each other and still could not quite understand what they were hearing.

Maples explained. "I want my company to have a man who is constantly thinking about how to help our employees become all they can be by living a balanced, healthy lifestyle. I think that man should be someone who has had to learn these principles himself. Clayton, I want you to be that man.

Clayton could not believe his ears. Maples went on. "You will be our CPO—Chief People Officer. You will be a full-fledged officer in our company with a substantial pay increase and perks. Now, as your first act of duty as CPO, I direct you to get your wife into your car and go meet your son at the Dairy Queen."

Clayton stammered and said, "Mr. Maples, I'm speechless. I can't believe you would show up at the end of the game and make an offer like this."

Maples said with a smile, "End of the game, you say? I didn't miss a pitch! I stood on the other side of the concession stand so you couldn't see me. Eddie's right fielder really should have caught that ball in the third inning. I thought Eddie's first at-bat

TIGHTROPE TANGO

was a good one. Didn't you think he was seeing the ball really well today?"

Clayton said, "Mr. Maples, you are amazing!"

With Mr. Maples' arms around Clayton and Darlene, they tangoed toward the car and into their happily balanced future.

Conclusion

In this book, we've discussed why it is important to lead a balanced life and how you can achieve balance. You may not necessarily need all the tools in this book, but there is undoubtedly at least one or two that you can use to help you fast-track your progress.

So what's next? Congratulations! You've finished Tightrope Tango...but you're not done yet. This is just the beginning.

Now the real work begins. You've outlined your plan for improving the workflow of your life. It's time to implement the solution. We encourage you to return to the tools in these pages from time to time to remind yourself of the guiding principles, and also the importance of your endeavor.

Leading a balanced life doesn't just lead to a potential job promotion; there is a host of benefits, from your career to your family life to your own personal fulfillment. By applying the principles you have learned, you will find yourself laser-focused on your own success, and you will have the tools to get to where you want to go.

Thank you for reading and good luck!

"When you achieve complete congruence between your values and your goals, like a hand in a glove, you feel strong, happy, healthy, and fully integrated as a person.
You develop a kind of courage that makes you completely unafraid to make decisions and take action.
Your whole life improves when you begin living your life by the values that you most admire."

- BRIAN TRACY

About the Author

Ray D. Waters is a professional speaker, author, and syndicated columnist who has traveled around the world teaching people the principles needed to live the highest quality life possible. With a focus on work-life balance and leadership, Ray loves teaching people how to avoid the pitfalls that have derailed so many on their life journey. Ray is also an entrepreneur who has helped start successful for profit and not for profit businesses in the United States and Eastern Europe. Regardless of any title he may wear, Ray is quick to make it known that his life's work is helping people.

Ray loves motivating individuals and organizations to become better and more productive than they ever imagined. His communication style is conversational, entertaining and authentic. He is known for the warm and engaging way he connects with audiences small and large.

Ray lives in Atlanta, Georgia with his wife Jane, who is his best friend. They are the proud parents of three grown children and six beautiful grandchildren, who affectionately call them Big and Mimi. Ray is also passionate about his role as the founder and lead teacher at The Village Church, an inter-denominational church in South Atlanta.

Visit Ray on his website at www.RayWaters.com. For speaking engagements, seminars or keynote presentations on this or other topics, write Ray at Ray@RayWaters.com or call him at 404-969-5519.

References

"About Emotional Intelligence." TalentSmart, n.d. Web. 2013. <http://www.talentsmart.com/about/emotional-intelligence.php>

Bandura, Albert. *Social Learning Theory*. New Jersey: Prentice Hall, 1977.

Drucker, Peter F. *The Practice of Management*. New York: Harper & Row, Publishers, Inc., 1993.

"Healthy Eating, Exercise Linked with Workplace Productivity." Huffington Post, 12 August, 2012. Web. 2013.

Monadjem, A.M. Seven Successes of Smarter Teams. 2012.

Prati, L. Melita. "Emotional Intelligence, Leadership Effectiveness, and Team outcomes." *The International Journal of Organizational Analysis*, Vol. 11, No. 1. 2003: 21-40.

Ramsey, Dave. *The Total Money Makeover: A Proven Plan for Financial Fitness.* Nashville: Thomas Nelson, Inc., 2003.

Schmitt, Emily. "How A Flexible Work Schedule Can Help You Strike The Balance." Forbes, 16 March, 2009. Web. 2013.

Sinek, Simon. *Start with Why: How Great Leaders Inspire Everyone to Take Action*. New York: Penguin Group, 2009.

Tsotsis, Alexia. "Google's '20 Percent Time' Will Survive The Death of Google Labs." TechCrunch, 20 July, 2011. Web. 2013.

U.S. Department of Health and Human Services. <u>The Health Consequences of Smoking: A Report of the Surgeon</u>

General. Atlanta: U.S. Department of Health and Human Services, Centers for Disease Control and Prevention, National Center for Chronic Disease Prevention and Health Promotion, Office on Smoking and Health, 2004

Analytical Insights

Steven Covey – Educator, executive, keynote speaker and bestselling author of *The Seven Habits of Highly Effective People.*

Orrin Woodward – Author and trainer. Co-author of the New York Times bestseller *Launching a Leadership Revolution* and many other critically acclaimed leadership and personal development books.

Timothy Ferriss – Author, entrepreneur and public speaker. Author of *The 4-Hour Work Week, The 4-Hour Body and The 4-Hour Chef,* all New York Times Best Sellers.

Ike Reighard – CEO, CPO, author, pastor and inspirational speaker. Author of *Treasures From The Dark, Discovering Your North Star and Discovering Your North Star Journal.* He is co-author of *Daily Insights,* with the late Zig Ziglar and co-author of *Tightrope Tango* with Ray D. Waters.

John Sununu – Governor of New Hampshire (1983-1989) and later the White House Chief of Staff under President George H. W. Bush.

Harvey Mackay – Executive and columnist who is best known as the author of five business bestsellers, including *Swim With the Sharks (Without Being Eaten Alive), Beware the Naked Man Who Offers You His Shirt* and *Dig Your Well Before You're Thirsty.* He is a nationally syndicated columnist, and one of America's most popular business speakers.

Tom Hopkins – Professional speaker, author and trainer. Tom has authored twelve books, including *Selling for Dummies* and *How to Master the Art of Selling,* which has sold over 1.4 million copies and is translated into ten languages.

Zig Ziglar – Author, salesman, and motivational speaker. Ten of his twenty-eight books have been on the best seller lists, and his titles have been translated into more than thirty-eight languages and dialects.

Lee Iacocca – Executive known for engineering the Ford Mustang and Ford Pinto cars. He served as President and CEO of Chrysler from 1978 and additionally as chairman from 1979, until his retirement at the end of 1992.

Natasha Munson – Author, inspirational speaker, writing coach and CEO of Be Magic, Inc., a nonprofit organization dedicated to empowering single mothers and their children. She published and co-authored «*Life Lessons for My Beautiful Black Girls.*»

Jim Rohn – Entrepreneur, author and motivational speaker.

Og Mandino – Author of *The Greatest Salesman in the World.* His books have sold over 50 million copies and have been translated into over twenty-five different languages. He was the president of Success Unlimited magazine until 1976 and is an inductee of the National Speakers Association's Hall of Fame.

Ralph Waldo Emerson – Essayist, lecturer, and poet.

Brian Tracy – Motivational speaker and author. He has conducted seminars and workshops in 61 countries worldwide, and is the Chairman and CEO of Brian Tracy International, a company specializing in the training and development of individuals and organizations.